CW01418494

FROM NERD

TO KNIGHT

The Story of a Traveler of the Jedi Way

FROM NERD TO KNIGHT
The Story of a Traveler of the Jedi Way

BY
Jared Avery Michaels

Copyright © 2012 Jared A. Michaels
ALL RIGHTS RESERVED

No part of this book may be reproduced, stored in a retrievable system or transmitted in any way by any means, be they electronic, mechanical, photocopy, recording or otherwise, without written consent of the author, except where permitted by United States Copyright Law.

Neither this book nor its content have been prepared, endorsed or approved by or affiliated in any way with George Lucas or Lucasfilm Ltd., or any other person or entity affiliated with Lucasfilm, *Star Wars*, or related properties. The opinions and ideas contained herein are solely those of the author, unless otherwise noted.   Star Wars, and its many subsequent characters and trademarks, are the property of Lucasfilm Ltd.

DEDICATION

To all those who have guided me down my path, knowingly or otherwise. To Dewayne, who is now one with the Force.

For Kharis

《》《》《》《》《》

INTRODUCTION

WHAT IS A JEDI? A very good question, but as it is with most things, the explanation is usually far less than the truth. Words are so limiting that way. This question I, and those like me, have been trying to answer and understand now for many years. There are several others out there on the path, but none of us have a good answer for you. Often times on the Jedi Way, and pretty much any religio-philisophical path to be honest, those on the path do not have an answer, they must simply strive to be the answer. By this, it is to say that there is no answer that can be put into words. Just as the opening line of the *Tao Te Ching*:

"The Tao that can be named is not the Eternal Tao."

We are people, just like you, who have found a spark of truth locked in a world of fiction. And, why not? The fiction was based on many world-accepted truths, mostly Taoist in nature, but some other points as well. George Lucas, creator of *Star Wars* and the basic structure of the Jedi Path, stated once that he created the Jedi to make people think about God. Now, of course, that is paraphrased, but this implies that he created the Jedi Path to make people more spiritually conscious. It worked, possibly far more

1

than he intended. The idea permeated society so deeply, I personally can't help but wonder if the spark for the creation of this esoteric space-sect wasn't divinely inspired somehow. *I want to make sure that it is clearly stated that the previous statement is just a thought that flows through my head from time to time. It is not the supported idea of the movement as a whole.* In truth, I am not even sure I believe it, just question it is all.

Back to the point, the Jedi were created to bring about a renewed spiritual awareness, written in the 1970s, when such sentiment still ran high in the youth of America. New ideas popped up all the time, some of them blends of several paths, others just retoolings of primarily one path. Either way, it happened, and when it hit the silver screen, there was no stopping it.

There is no telling how many lives George changed with this. People say *Star Wars* changed the movie-making industry as we know it, but I say it changed a great deal more than that. I know many people who would agree: it changed the face of spirituality on this planet far more than how movies get made.

Enough of my adoration for this man's vision and creation, no matter how fascinating it is to think about. This book is designed to show how a person can develop from what people consider "normal" into someone who found his faith in fiction. I have laid out this text to aid with that as best I can.

You will notice the chapters change in tone. Some are childish, some angry, some sporadic. It is all intentionally done so as to help the reader better see what exactly I was going through at each point in the story. It is to show the steps I made, both forward and backward, along the Way.

After each chapter, there will be a list of the most influential revelations that I have experienced, even if I did not talk about them directly in the chapter. Most of the listed articles will be my own, but some will not. In fact, most of the earlier ones will be what I have archived of the work of others over the years. This way, you as the reader, can see my growth in the Jedi Way, whether the revelation is inherently Jedi or not.

I ask each of you, no matter how doubting you may be in what you are reading, please just take the time and, as Bruce Lee was fond of saying, empty your cup to allow new ideas to flow in. If in the end, you do not agree with me, that is fine. I am not writing this to convert people to the Jedi Way as I see it, simply to tell my tale, so that those who may be looking can find it. If I only confer one tiny sliver of understanding to you, the reader, then my work was not in vain.

Please also note, I am not doing this to make myself look good. I am actually a pretty terrible role model for most of the tale. I still consider myself a pretty bad example of what to do, and how to do it. I write this partly as an explanation, partly as a cautionary lesson. Either way, the events are as truthful as I can remember them.

On with the tale...

J. A. MICHAELS

《》《》《》《》《》

FIRST STEPS INTO A MUCH LARGER WORLD

As I grow older, I lose more and more of my childhood memories. Most of them are trivial, like the first fortune cookie I ever got was in elementary school, and said, "One day you will be rich and famous". It hasn't happened so far, but I still have the fortune. Some are unpleasant, like when I was still riding a tricycle, my older brother was pushing me up the driveway, and the wheel cut sideways. I fell face first onto the driveway and cracked a tooth. I still remember the lower part hanging by a thin piece of enamel. There were some good times, there, too. I remember swimming, and playing with frogs that came into the back yard. I remember the first bull whip I ever held, and cracking it in the front yard like Zorro. I remember standing in the lunch line in kindergarten the first time I realized I had internal dialog. I felt so amazed that I could speak without sound, and wondered if anyone else could, too. Other than that, I remember learning about Hanukkah in school, and taking a few months of tae-kwon-do the summer I turned eight.

Mostly, though, I remember how I felt. I was the typical chubby kid in school. I was shy about my weight, and can't remember ever having more than two friends at a time all through school. I was awkward and clumsy, and pretty much just stayed to myself. No one really tired to talk to me much anyway, so it worked out. Mostly, my home life faltered, too. My parents fought a lot with each other, and I fought a lot with my brothers. We learned to be mean from our Dad, and at least I learned to be silently defiant from my Mom. I was diagnosed with ADD, Attention Deficit Disorder, in the fifth grade, I remember being put on the kiddie cure-all of the time, Ritalin. I remember, not very well, being a zombie of my former self, and never having an appetite. I am sure as my intake lessened, the lack of hunger a side-effect of my medication, the zombie state was enhanced by a lack of metabolic fuel. I remember being told ADD was a short circuit in my brain, so it didn't work right. Great thing to tell a ten year-old with low self-esteem, right?

One thing I will never forget, though, is finding *Star Wars*. I was about twelve or so, and I had been hearing all the hype about the upcoming Special Edition re-release of the original trilogy. I also remember, at the time, hating *Star Wars*. Other than the cool weapons, I hated everything about it. I was a Trekkie, through and through. *Star Wars* was too complex for me at the time, too convenient. Things happened just at the right instant for everyone to be okay. Truth be told, at the point the Special Editions were coming out, I couldn't actually remember the story at all. All I knew was that Luke got his hand cut off, Darth Vader was Luke's father, and they had really awesome weapons. Finally, I got fed up with all the hype, and decided it was time to figure out, once and for all, what the big deal was.

I remember digging through box after box of old VHS tapes, and eventually finding a copy of *Star Wars Episode IV: A New Hope* my parents had recorded off TV who knows how many years before. I remember getting frustrated with the constant Isotoner Glove commercials that littered the recording. Obviously, the original broadcast had been around Christmas time. Way-too-many commercials or not, I was instantly hooked on the story. The characters were all so fresh and alive. They all played together in a peculiar harmony of humor, action, and mystique.

So I asked my Dad, well begged and pestered are likely more accurate terms, to purchase the entire trilogy for me. He bought me the Original Release Widescreen VHS Collector's Box Set. I still have it, come to think of it. I was so excited, I watched them all in one day. The only problem was, well, I watched them out of order. Episodes IV, VI, and then V. They were placed in the box in the wrong order, and I didn't know any better. It didn't matter, either. Context clues kind of helped me piece it all together. Watching Yoda die, then watching Luke find Yoda, that part really helped. Oh, wow! What a change in me! I was excited to watch them again and again and again. I watched them so often that I could hear just a sound clip, not even words, and tell you what movie, and what approximate area it was in.

I wanted to get it all, the awesome black uniform, the great flowing robe, and the heft of a lightsaber hanging off my belt.

I remember going out into the garage and digging through my Dad's junk drawers. He has worked in construction all his life. Carpenter, electrician, elevator repair. He had tools, and pipes, and fittings, and a freakishly diverse slew of other little odds and ends. I remember fitting together, made of a wide variety of conduit couplings and a few other pipe fittings, my first prop lightsaber hilt. It is heavy, and clunky. There are no guts in it. You can even look straight through it, as the end piece I found did not close it off. I didn't care. It was a lightsaber, and it was mine. And, yes, I still have that, too.

By the time this happened, my parents had divorced, and I remember going to the condo my Mom and her then-boyfriend were living in, and getting on her computer to look up pictures from *Star Wars*. I remember that I was looking specifically from a picture of Mark Hamill, dressed in his character's trademark all-black with one glove, green lightsaber blazing endlessly into the darkness, preferably with the little gray section showing on his chest. This was before the rise of the internet giant, Google. I remember getting on HotBot, a search engine eventually bought, then shut down by Lycos. It was crude by today's standards, but I am so glad it was.

I was looking for just one more awesome picture of Luke for the day, when I ran across a website that caught my eye, and changed my outlook on the world forever. This site was called Kharis Nightflyer's Jedi Praxeum. It spoke of something a fanatic teenager would never have thought of, but could not turn away from.

It spoke of **becoming a real Jedi!**

In hindsight, the website and its information base was pretty weak. There was a basic breathing technique, a very basic sensing meditation technique, an early time line of the *Star Wars* universe, a little blurb about the fictional technology behind a lightsaber, and an article about the dangers of teaching these things to other people. I didn't care how thin it all was then, and I don't really mind it now. That was the vibe of the day. We all had our roots as fans first, and Jedi second. We were young, both in physical age and in maturity of the Way. Thinking back, we were all so starry-eyed for something so small to spark such awe. It didn't matter though. It is said there are many paths to the top of the mountain. For me, and the countless others who started their journey at Kharis's digital school, it was enough. Truth be told, if the site had been any larger, I likely would not have even looked at it.

I remember sitting down in the bedroom my brothers and I shared when we were at Mom's for the weekend, on a big pillow, and meditating for the first time in my life. I had my prized lightsaber prop sitting on the floor in front of me, and I stared at it for a long time. I remember trying to reach out with my feelings, as I had heard so many times in the films, and to feel my lightsaber prop. I also remember feeling for the first time, the lightest trickle of what I would soon learn was the Force.

Now, the Force has always been part of life, it has just worn many names throughout history. Qi, prana, magick, mana, god-force, bioelectricity. The list is nearly endless. Call it what you will, I am Jedi, and I call it the Force. It all works the same way, at its core. Calm and focus your mind, open yourself to an energy greater than yourself, feel the spark of life grow in every cell, and direct the energy to a desired action.

Back to the story, at that point, I had no idea what it was. I thought I might have imagined feeling my lightsaber hilt without touching it. At the time, this thing was like a security blanket for me. Aside from school, it never left my side. Even now, so many years later, I still know the feel of its weight in my hand. So, I doubted it, as any jaded little teenager would do. But, doubt or not, I could not pass on the possibility. I went into the living room where my Mom and future Step-Dad were sitting, and asked my Mom to hide my lightsaber from me. I went back into the bedroom, and shut the door. It was do or die time. If it didn't work, I would throw it all down the tubes. If it did work... It wouldn't work... It couldn't work... Could it?

I remember asking myself if I was an idiot for believing in such a thing, so mystical energy that I, a normal person, could harness. I was a good little Baptist kid then, went to church on Sunday's with my grandmom, just like I was supposed to, ya know? I love those memories of church with her. It is from her I learned the true power of faith, and that lesson would stick with me forever. But here I was, playing with a power I did not know, and never read in my Bible being offered to anyone but Moses, a gift of God. I didn't pray, or ask for God's help. I just knew I was playing with a spark. It would either catch fire, or leave me cold.

Mom comes back to the bedroom and tells me it's hidden. I follow her into the living room, and stand in the middle with my eyes closed, and tried to remember what my lightsaber hilt felt like. I remember being a little embarrassed standing there, hoping I could find something without seeing it, or overturning things looking for it. No logic, just a quiet mind, and a stretching of the senses. Then, I felt it. I felt it sure as I feel the keys I am typing this on now. I moved to where the feeling was. I could feel it under the chair my Mom's boyfriend was sitting in while fixing something on his computer. I pulled back the sheet he had over the chair to pick it up off the ground and...

It wasn't there. But I knew I felt it. So, I went to a different part of the room, and felt it coming from there again. I *knew* I felt it. I knew it wasn't all in my head, but no matter how hard I looked, it wasn't there. Whether I knew it or not, I felt my hilt somewhere that it wasn't. I looked under the chair, taped to the bottom of the chair, under the edge of the table right at the chair, on top of the table. It was nowhere that I looked. I remember finally crushing under the weight of this realization, allowing my frustration and embarrassment to get the better of me.

I gave up, about to beat myself up for even imagining such things might be true. When I asked for my prop back, my Mom's boyfriend stood up and handed me my lightsaber. He had been sitting on it the whole time! I remember feeling the hilt tingle when it slapped my palm. I looked at my Mom, and she looked both a little amazed and amused. She says she has forgotten the incident by now, but it will never leave my mind.

It had worked. It had really worked! The Force had worked! The Force was with me! Sure, It wasn't the sharpest sensation in the world, but I was on my first trial run. It was okay that I didn't get it exact, I knew it was there, and I knew it worked!

It was that day, so many years ago, that I stepped onto the Jedi Way, taking *my* first steps into a much larger worldview, one that included the Force. It was that day that I knew, with all certainty, I would walk this world a Jedi.

I went back to Dad's at the end of the weekend, and remember feeling all sorts of new things. I remember looking into the night sky in Memphis, where I have lived all my life, and feeling a sense of confusion and wonder and fear. I cannot remember a time in my life I had ever felt so large, or so small. I remember checking my pocket one more time, making sure the pages my Mom printed off for me, the Calming Breath Technique, and the Lesson on Meditation, were still there. I remember closing my eyes and feeling my lightsaber hilt humming a note only I could feel in my bag, closed up safely in the trunk of the car. It was going to be such an awesome ride. I remember working on the Calming Breath at school for the next few weeks, working it until it was almost automatic. Honing the rough edges off the technique until, just like Kharis said I would, it became so smooth no one noticed I was doing it. I remember standing in the back yard and playing with the wind. I would feel the Force in my hand, and wave my hand a certain way, and a breeze would fly in from that angle. It amazed me how easy it all was, with the right perspective. I even remember stopping the wind several times when I was cutting the grass and it was blowing the grass clippings in my eyes. I worked on the meditation technique, focusing each time on my lightsaber hilt, that I had built with my own hands, knowing its every bump and dent, committing its existence to some internal memory that I didn't know existed some weeks before.

Now, please remember as you read this, we were all so young in this path, so fresh to it, we held onto any symbol we could to keep it with us. I think, in the back of my mind, I felt that my heavy piece of tubing and fittings was my only way to be the Jedi I was searching to become. Educated just by the movies at that point, all I knew was you learned to touch the Force, almost see with it. Then, you learned to sense things with it, and feel things about the future. Then you worked out to make yourself stronger. And finally, you dressed in all black and bit down on your emotions. **That** was the largest part of my example back then. A few books had come out, but very few explored the philosophical aspect at all. And those were way beyond my reading level at that point, anyway.

We. I say it because I know in hindsight I was not alone in this journey, but at the time I thought it was just me and Kharis, the only two Jedi in the world. He was like Old Ben, and I was Luke. We were training to defend the world from evil.

Lesson One: The Force

-The Force is what gives a Jedi his power. It's an energy field created by all living things. It surrounds us and penetrates us. It binds the galaxy together.

-For over a thousand generations the Jedi Knights were the guardians of peace and justice in the Old Republic. Before the dark times, before the Empire.

------Obi Wan Kenobi

-Concentrate. Feel the Force flow. Not outside or inside, but part of all it is. Through the Force, things you will see. Reaches across time and space it does. Other places. The future... the past. Old friends long gone. Always in motion is the future.

-Size matters not. Look at me. Judge me by my size, do you? And well you should not. For my ally is the Force. And a powerful ally it is. Life creates it, makes it grow. Its energy surrounds us and binds us. Luminous beings are we... not this crude matter. You must feel the Force around you. Here, between you... me... the tree... the rock... everywhere!

-In balance is the Force. The Dark and the Light. With out one, there is no other. The Dark Side, tempting it is. Quick, easy at first, but a trap is the Dark Side. Corrupting, evil. Once you start down the Dark path, forever will it dominate your destiny. For the Light Side, patience you need. Control. Peace and harmony it is.

------Yoda

Lesson Two: The Path of Darkness

Does the Force use the Jedi, or the Jedi use the Force? To use the Force, one must be at harmony with it. Only when calm, at peace, can one act with assurance of control. When one is at harmony with the universe, one acts as one must to maintain harmony. The will and the Force are one; the actor and the acted upon, the same. There is no contradiction: there is unity. That is the path of Light.

There is another – the path of Darkness.

The universe is an angry morass of power. To release that power, one must harness one's basest emotions: hate, anger, fear, aggression. By releasing one's own anger, one releases the anger of eternity. Only when filled with hate, can one perform the most hateful of acts. The will and the Force are one.

That is the choice of the Jedi: serenity or hatred; peace or anger; freedom or tyranny; learning or power; the Light or the Darkness.

Because the use of the Force and the way the Force uses its user are one, the choice is inescapable. A Jedi who starts down the path of the Dark Side will forever be dominated by it. That is why the Jedi must follow a strict code.

Lesson Three: The Nature of the Force

From lifelessness came life; from dead matter came spirit. With life came perception: the perception of beauty and ugliness, serenity and fear. The Force grew strong as life grew stronger. Life is the universe's way of perceiving itself; the Force is the strength of its perception.

As life grew, evolved, became more sophisticated, there came intelligence – and with it, the capacity of understanding. Intelligent beings questioned the universe, and when they were clever enough to ask the questions in the right way, the universe answered. The Force became stronger, more sophisticated, as intelligence spread and sapient's knowledge of the universe deepened.

Yet the nature of the Force is hidden and subtle. Questions about the nature of matter and energy are more easily answered. Intelligent beings developed a high technology by understanding of physical law – yet understanding of the universe's mystical nature lagged behind. Intelligent beings built advanced cultures which were cold, cruel, ignorant of the beat of reality's heart.

So stood the galaxy, until the rise of the Jedi. They studied the Force; they took first few steps on the road to universal harmony. As their mastery deepened, as their fame spread, and as their works began to bring harmony and freedom to the galaxy, they were betrayed.

For the Force is not itself good or evil; it is a reflection of nature, and nature itself can be cold and cruel. Evil ones can harness the force to their will – and, by doing so, lose something of their humanity, becoming virtual avatars of the Dark Side of the Force. For the Master of the Dark Side, as for a Master of the Light, it cannot be said whether one controls the Force, or the Force the Master; to ask which is the actor and which the acted upon is a question of no meaning.

It was inevitable that some would use the Force to slake their base lust for wealth and power. The Dark Side is easy and seductive; the first successes brought thirst for more. These evil ones brought the great Jedi low, hunting down and killing all of their ancient order.

All – or almost all.

Lesson Four: The Jedi Code

There is no emotion; there is peace.
There is no ignorance; there is knowledge.
There is no passion; there is serenity.
There is no death; there is the Force.

To use the Force, the Jedi must remain at harmony with it. To act in dissonance depletes one's power. The Force is created and sustained by life. The Jedi acts to preserve life. To kill is wrong. Yet it is often necessary to kill. The Jedi may kill in self defense or the defense of others. You may kill if, by doing so, life is preserved.

But you must know, always, that killing is wrong. When you kill, you commit a crime against the Force. Though you may know that you do so for the greater good, and the greater good justifies your act, you must also know that the death remains as a stain upon your spirit.

The Jedi does not act for personal gain, of wealth or of power. You must act to gain knowledge; to sustain freedom, life, and learning; to defeat those who would impose tyranny, death and ignorance.

Sometimes, wealth or power is needed to achieve the Jedi's goals. Money is required for the purchase of goods; power is required to obtain the help of others. To achieve one's goals, a Jedi may obtain wealth or power, but is not interested in it for its own sake, and will surrender it once those goals are achieved.

A Jedi never acts from hatred, anger, fear or aggression. A Jedi must act when calm, at peace with the Force. To act from anger is to court the Dark Side, to risk everything for which the Jedi stand.

Lesson Five: A Jedi's Greatest Ally
A Jedi's greatest ally is the Force.

The Jedi's use of the Force is his greatest skill and most difficult achievement. The Force is a powerful field created by all living things; it surrounds and penetrates the entire galaxy ...but it does not fall to everyone to use it as a source of insight and power.

A Jedi from the beginning must do what most men cannot; develop a sensitivity to this Force. He must actually feel it, feel his oneness with it, feel it tangible flow through him, then his conscious awareness must join the Force so that the knowledge through the Force will become his own.

At some point a Jedi learns to abandon reliance on his own mind and its effort. He learns to stretch out with his feeling , to let go of his limited idea of himself, and to move with the deeply instinctive levels of his being. By listening, by becoming peaceful, by turning his attention to the Force, he finds that place where his individuality is joined to the knowledge and power of the universe.

At some point a Jedi becomes one with the force. It consumes him, penetrates him, makes him part of all living things.

Lesson Six: The Nature of the Dark Side

Unlike the Light Side of the Force, which embraces the whole, the entire focus of the Dark Side is the self. The appeal of the Dark Side is its very destructiveness and its isolation. Those who seek power for selfish reasons find comfort in its narcissistic gaze. The Dark Side emphasizes aggrandizement of self to the exclusion of others. In this way, rage and anger are turned into sources of strength.

Many are attracted to the Dark Side because its selfish nature allows great and showy deeds. The ease with which power is summoned belies its danger, for anger and hatred consume the individual even as one dominates one's surroundings. Ultimately, the Dark Side rejects the very celestial nature of life itself. To the Jedi, the Force is not a part of their existence; it is their existence. To a student of the Dark Side, this is incomprehensible.

It is not uncommon for Dark Side students to go into the wilderness, much as their Light Side counterparts do. The crucial difference is that the Light Jedi goes into the wilderness to commune with the wild. The Dark Side follower goes to separate himself from the community of life. There, in isolation, a Dark Side follower can perfect his or her own oneness with the Dark Side, and revel in that corruption. Yet in the Dark Side are anger and hatred and isolation and...fear. That fear drives the Jedi to isolation, jealousy and desire to be the most powerful of all.

This very predatory nature sparks battles of dominance when several Dark Jedi or Dark Side Adepts gather. Sometimes these are violent confrontations, other times they involve subtle mind games or diplomatic discussions; but make no mistake, there will be some attempt to assert control over each other. The violent nature of the Dark Side often leads to betrayal and bloodshed.

Not only does this fratricidal tendency discourage long term cooperation among Adepts, it has also hindered the passing of knowledge. Whereas the Jedi and other servants of the Light Side have established great libraries and oral traditions to advance their work and educate succeeding generations, those of the Dark Side have few such institutions. Many never record their knowledge for fear it may aid an enemy. Others are too arrogant to allow others to learn from their mistakes.

Lesson Seven: Aspects of Light and Dark

The ancient mystics of the galaxy have long studied the omnipresent nature of the Force. These scholars and philosophers discovered that the Force was the essence of the universe's cycle of existence, part of life and death in nature. All things in existence are a part of it, but none so much as living, sapient beings. They further learned that with years of patient study, the Force could eventually be manipulated by individuals in a way that defied rational explanations. Because the Force is everywhere, there are no limits to the feats that could be achieved if the being using the Force was knowledgeable enough of its way. Beings could communicate across vast distances, heighten their senses and see past the veils of time.

These learned ones preserved their knowledge and established traditions to train their descendants and increase their understanding. These great traditions of enlightenment came to flourish across the galaxy. Many of them focused on particular qualities of the Force or on different disciplines that were but one of many ways of knowing the Force. Still, most of these scholars do agree on basic principles. To better understand the ways of the Force, these scholars characterized it by its two most fundamental aspects: the Light Side and the Dark Side.

The Light is positive. It is intimately bound with the essence of living things; it is peace, harmony, and knowledge. The Light Side springs from the great pattern of existence. It draws strength from diversity and tolerance. It is also inherently communal in nature, thriving on cooperation. Those emotions that enhance the existence of the whole flow from it and tap into its great reserves of strength and peace. Patience, humility, and self-sacrifice are paths to enlightenment. Above all, it seeks harmony and perfection.

The Dark Side, in comparison, is the force of entropy and destruction. Chaos and rage feed it and are its sources of power. The Dark Side is a part of nature--it is not inherently evil, but evil comes from its irrationality, its intolerance, and its lack of control. Bestial and predatory, domination is its goal. Mercilessly aggressive and unforgiving, its adherents are blinded by greed and lust for power over those weaker than themselves.

The Light and Dark Side manifest themselves in the way they are used; they are simply different interpretations of a single aspect of nature, and they exist in balance with themselves and the universe.

Just as with any aspect of life and death, both the Dark Side and the Light Side are intertwined with each other, are necessary to each other and form a cosmic balance. The important matter is avoiding the emotions of anger and hate which summon the Dark Side. By concentration, it is possible to go beyond desire and emotion, and thereby grow very powerful in the Light Side of the Force. Then great things are possible.

Lesson One: Calming Breath Technique

This is a simple breathing exercise, to be practiced every day. It is useful in stressful situations, or when you feel threatened, for it helps you to remain calm, and to relax. It is presented in three easy steps. Start with the first step, until you've mastered it. Then progress to the next step. Once you have reached the third step, you will have learned the Calming Breath Technique.
Preparation

Wear loose fitting attire, so that you are comfortable. Make sure that you can breathe through your nose. If you have a cold, do not practice this exercise until you can breathe clearly.

<u>Step One</u>
Lie flat on your back. Put one hand on your stomach, and the other hand on your chest. Relax.

Inhale so that the hand on your stomach rises, while the hand on your chest is still. Exhale so that the hand on your stomach goes down again, and the hand on your chest remains still. Repeat for 5 breaths.

Now, when you inhale, breathe in so that the hand on your chest rises, while the hand on your stomach is still. Exhale so that the hand on your chest goes down again, while the hand on your stomach remains still. Repeat for 5 breaths.

Alternate between stomach and chest breathing for 5 minutes. Make sure you've mastered this step before moving on.

Step Two
This step combines stomach and chest breathing into one breath. This is the Calming Breath.

Lie flat on your back. Put one hand on your stomach, and the other hand on your chest. Relax.

Begin by stomach breathing. When you feel you can't inhale any more in this manner, switch to chest breathing, until the upper part of your lungs are filled. Then exhale by chest breathing first, progressing to stomach breathing so that you empty the lungs fully. Repeat for 5 minutes.

Breathe slowly. If you feel dizzy, slow down, you are breathing too fast. If you are out of breath, you are breathing too slowly. Listen to your own body's messages. If you are having difficulty distinguishing chest breathing from stomach breathing, go back to Step One.

Step Three
Stand or sit with your back straight.

Use the Calming Breath and follow this pattern. You will have to count the rhythm in your head. I will teach you the rhythm 4-4-4. Count to 4 while inhaling, hold your breath and count to 4, then count to 4 while exhaling. Once you've mastered this you may use a 4-4-4-4 rhythm is you prefer. It adds and extra step of holding your breath after exhaling and counting to 4. Take care not to hold your breath too long. Again, listen to your body. Repeat for 5 minutes, or until you are calm.

Practice so that the Calming Breath becomes effortless, and inaudible. You should breathe no louder than usual. Once you have mastered the technique, it should be invisible to the untrained eye, making it useful in almost any situation.

The calm mind can more readily feel the ebb and flow of the Force.

Lesson Two: Jedi Meditation – Basic Technique

Jedi meditation techniques have been handed down through the ages as a way of gaining insight and wisdom in the force. There were many different meditation techniques, but most have been lost to the ravages of time. The following is the first step in the most commonly practiced method.

Like all force training, the Jedi meditation technique follows a hierarchy of steps: Control, Sense, and Alter. You must learn control of your own abilities, before you can truly sense the Force. Once you have mastered sensing the Force surrounding you, you can use the force to perform actions and alter the events and objects around you.

The basic technique teaches you to control your own mental process, and allows you to focus your thoughts on one object, thought, or goal, the object of your meditation. This object must have a clear objective or subjective reality to you, so it is easiest to begin with a physical object such as a ball or a candle. After you have mastered meditating on physical objects, you may proceed to mental objects such as mental images or goals. Make sure your mental object is clearly defined in your mind.

How to start:
–Sit in on the floor, or on a cushion, with the spine and neck kept straight . Place your hands in your lap, palms upward.
–Relax your entire body deeply and quickly, using the Calming Breath Technique. After you are relaxed, regulate your breathing to a calm and peaceful rate.

-If you are using a physical object, focus your vision on the object, otherwise close your eyes.

-Begin to shut out distractions (noises, etc.), as you focus your attention inward. Try to keep your thoughts from wandering, shutting out stray thoughts.

-Concentrate your thoughts upon the object of your meditation.

Practice these steps until you are able to concentrate on the object without distraction. Once you have mastered these steps, you should gain a sense of that object through the Force. Stretch out with your feelings, and perceive the object.

Lesson Three: A Jedi's First Battle

A Jedi's first true battle is with oneself, and no one else. Only when you have done this can you truly become a Jedi.

"You cannot control it, you will be tempted! Don't give into hate it leads to the dark side."

One of the major themes running throughout Master Skywalker's tale is Luke's battle with himself. Luke finally won the battle when faced with killing his own father, he said no and turned away from the dark side of the force. At this point the emperor knew that he was lost to the Dark side and decided to have him killed. Luke had to overcome the hatred, fear and anger (emotions of the dark side) he felt toward his father and forgive him for all that he had done (destroyed the Jedi, tortured his friends, killing Ben, though probably most importantly abandoning Luke as a child and failing to be a father to him).

Fighting the battle with the darkness within was the lesson of the tree where the dark side was strong. When Luke entered he asked "What is in there?" and Yoda replied "Only what you take with you." In other words the tree merely reflected and brought out the place were the dark side resided within Luke, that is his feeling towards his father. Striking Darth Vader down in the tree, signified Luke killing himself or more importantly failing the test of a Jedi to turn away from the Dark side. As already mentioned, when Luke latter forgave his father and refused to kill his father he successfully turned away from the Dark side.

If you wish to become a Jedi, you must face those places of pain, anger and mistrust within you, places where the dark side of the force grows and lingers. You must forgive those that have harmed you in the past and truly Love them. For unless you do this, no matter how much physical and mental training you will do you will be at risk of falling to the ways of the Dark Side. You must first battle the foe within before you can help others.

May the Force be with you...

The Dangers of Training Jedi

"Training Jedi is a most rewarding pursuit, but one ringed with many unseen perils. Never, oh Master Jedi, rest easy when your pupil begins to grow anxious to learn at a pace greater than that which you have set for him. Such impatience is natural in the young and inexperienced, and a commendable trait in a student. But it also signals a time when the pupil is most open to the temptation of stepping into the broad path of instant gratification and easy advancement that leads to the dark side. Beware, Jedi Master, lest through carelessness and inattention you loose on the galaxy a monster..."

--Bodo Baas

The Ancient Jedi masters knew that Jedi training must proceed at a slow pace. Too much power gathered too quickly can corrupt even the most selfless and devout Jedi apprentice. A Jedi student must be properly humble in his powers, and mature enough to embrace the tremendous responsibility that comes with wielding the Force.

A student impatient with the slow pace of the tutorship, a gifted student eager to dispense with "pointless exercises" and embrace the true power of the Force misses the entire point of being a Jedi. The Jedi does not crave power, but seeks to serve others, without the expectation of becoming "great in the Force." The true Jedi is cautious, and reluctant to learn too much too quickly. Overeager students run a fearful risk of opening themselves up to the temptations of taking the deceptively easy path of the dark side.

In the days of the Old Republic, the Jedi teachers kept a careful watch on their apprentices, ever alert for the telltale signs of the headstrong apprentice who wanted more than they were ready for. Every Jedi disciple soon heard the dreadful cautionary tale of the gifted Jedi Exar Kun, and how he was lost to the dark side by the arrogant belief that he could embrace Sith teachings and not be dominated. If a great Jedi Knight could fall, their teachers told them, they themselves must tread with special care.

While Jedi teachers in the past could draw upon centuries of tradition an experience in training Jedi, I have fewer resources available to me. I regret that I have known less than I should of the tremendous dangers which arrise in training Jedi. In the early days of the Academy, I failed to anticipate certain problems with my star pupils Gantoris and Kyp Durron. Gantoris lost his life for my failings, and Kyp was almost lost to the dark side.

Rest assured that I have come out of those experiences with a new respect for the awesome responsibility that comes with being the teacher of a new generation of Jedi.

《》《》《》《》《》

THE COMMUNITY

Well, my thought of being the only student of the only Jedi in the world quickly faded. I soon ran out of sources of information. Kharis's website was so limited that it soon became a hindrance in my journey, so I bid it farewell, and went to the world wide web in search of other Jedi to meet and learn from. That was when I found another place dedicated to the teaching of the Jedi. It was light years beyond Kharis's humble Praxeum, and it was staffed by not one, but five Jedi.

This was JediAcademy.com, lead by a man we all called Baal Legato. He was assisted by several others whom time has erased the names of. This place was vibrant and alive, its content evolving and growing, helping me down the Jedi Path. There was even a dark Jedi there who discussed the traps of the Jedi training, so that none who were not willing entered into the Dark Side. It had everything I thought I would ever need, until the day Baal set up something that changed the entire Jedi Path online.

He created a forum for everyone at the site to interact. In its first incarnation, the forum ran off a buggy guestbook script. It crashed at least twice a day, more than that usually. It was then that I realized the web of people I had entered into. The Force had come to more than just me. It made me feel more special, and less special, all at once.

We talked, we fought, we learned. We questioned, we answered, we shared. We grew. We were becoming Jedi. We were a community. We were the Jedi Community.

After a time, the guestbook forum finally died totally. Baal changed the face of the Community once again, casting the dye for a pattern that would never be undone. He found EzBoard, a web-forum server strong enough to handle us all. We had accounts, and could express ourselves with avatars and auto-signatures. We all became individuals in our quest. We could follow a conversation thread with ease, and could view a topic to decide if we wanted to comment on it or not. We had control of our path. The EzBoard became the standard for any Jedi website from that point onward, until it was bought by another site and shut down.

Oh, the people I met, and the things we did. The screen names we all saw: Koren Jey, Demetris Vorak, Rael Urn, Dark Lord Mal'Kith, Trad Davin, Rogue Ace, and countless others, all what we took as our Jedi Names. We all had the habit of hiding our birth names. Some did it to sever a tie between themselves and their former states of being, as an act of dedication to the Jedi Way. Some did it because they thought it was cool. Many did it just because it was what was done. The anonymity of the internet gave us this power to freely express ourselves on this new Path, and the safety of not being persecuted for it in the lives we were all escaping.

The most important part of this Community, though, was that it gave us other people to walk the path. I remember making fast friends with one such teen, like myself, named Jonathan. He and I became great friends, and to this day, I don't think I have ever met someone so sensitive. I remember one time in specific, Jonathan and I were talking over some instant messenger program. We were attempting to probe the mind of the other one, kind of just stealing a bit of their sight or hearing. We played this game back and forth for a while, some hits, some misses. I remember asking Jonathan to tell me what I was listening to. Whether I felt the pressure in my mind or not, I do not truly know. I do, however, know he blew me away when he said "children playing". I was listening to *Come Out and Play* by the Offspring. We were getting better, getting stronger. We were learning to use the Force not just to sense objects, or the future, but to catch impressions of other peoples' emotions and thoughts.

Aside from Jonathan, the one person I interacted with the most was a good friend indeed, the Grey Jedi Koren Jey. Koren was the first person to use that title that I had ever met. The Grey Jedi that he was is a revelation that most of us did not come to for years. He spoke of a balance between his Light and Dark emotions, because all those years ago, that was the model we had. He spoke of yin and yang, taking a symbol most of us never took the time to study, and made it part of his journey. Koren was a student of tai chi chuan, an internal Chinese martial art. He knew many of the principles of the tai chi player, and knew there was something not quite right in the stoic approach many of us attempted to take to the Jedi Way. He was also one of the largest proponents of the martial arts as a dedicated part of Jedi training, to replace the fantastical focus on lightsaber training.

We became big, real, alive. This caused a great deal of learning, and a great deal of problems. It brought us all to a level of personal pride, being able to share insight, and argue ideas. We all became slaves to our young growing egos. We fought often over terminology, rather than seeing the larger picture. Some still to this day are trapped in that problem, but we cannot all be at the same point on the Path, or we would all stagnate.

After a little over a year at the Academy, I stumbled upon yet another avenue of personal discovery into the Jedi Path, once more thanks to George Lucas and team.

《》《》《》《》《》

ENTER THE MEDIA

The introduction of the 1995 Game of the Year, *Dark Forces 2: Jedi Knight*, was just as much a turning point for me as it was for many others. Jedi could be found playing the multiplayer function of the game at any hour of the day, and countless more played through the solo adventures with gusto, milking any revelation into the Path we could. It was the first time I can remember anyone using the term "Light Side", be it in the various *Star Wars* media, or the Community itself, outside of Koren that is.

The game followed a man who discovered his ability to use the Force guiding himself down the path of self-discovery to become a Jedi. The game showed me that being of the Light or Dark was not a matter of grand perspective, but in how we acted all the time. Before the character ever touches the Force, or finds his lightsaber, if the player aimlessly kills non-combatants, his aspect is shifted to the Dark Side, and he has no control when the trial arrives as to what he can do. The character is stained, and becomes as bad as those he combats.

I remember having a close affinity to one of the characters in the game, a Dark Jedi student named Yun. He was dark by circumstance, but he was not totally evil. After the player defeats him, then spares his life, Yun is moved by his restraint and forgiveness, and eventually sacrifices himself to save the character from being killed while unconscious. I saw much of my own strife in him, fighting dark circumstances to overcome those around him pressuring him to be less than he could be, to the point that when I made my first set of Jedi robes, a practice of the early movement, I patterned them greatly after his.

We all saw what the Force could do, and we all got to interact in a more physical real-time game. I vividly remember both within the MSN Gaming Zone, the largest multiplayer server of the time, and in the game itself, often finding other Jedi, and those who desired to be Jedi. I asked them all to join the Academy, though few ever did for more than a moment. I also played as Yun while in multiplayer mode.

It was about this time that I also began reading for pleasure, another gift this Path has given me that changed my life in untold ways. I began by reading Kevin J. Anderson's *Young Jedi Knight* books. Lessons given to Jacen and Jaina were swallowed quickly, and read time and again, so that I could get the point of the lesson. I remember one such tale where the Jedi students were told they could build strength in more than one way: by lifting one heavy thing a hundred times, or by lifting a hundred heavy things only once. I know, its not a terribly profound lesson, but it was to me.

This quickly evolved into Anderson's *Jedi Academy* Trilogy, and Michael A. Stackpole's *I, Jedi*. Not to get out of time line here, but Stackpole's *I, Jedi* is by and far, the single greatest work on my development on this path. It is unparalleled in the insight it gave into the trials of one training to be Jedi. True enough, they are also fun stories to read, but that is not the reason I read the book so much that I had to by a second hardcover copy of it. I nearly destroyed my first hardcover copy. I know I lost the cover for it many years ago. It is worn, and the gold paint on the spine is faded in many places, missing in others. Perhaps a little on the fanatical side, but I cherish my worn copy as a priest cherishes their first Bible. Say what you will, but don't judge me too harshly.

The games and books became like Aesop's fables for me, and many others like me. We finally had a more complete example to follow. It was in Anderson's works that many of us found the Jedi Code, though I learned much later it was written for some card game several years prior. Luke, Leia, Callista, Corran, Kam, Kyp, Gantoris, Streen, Mara, and Tamith Kai all became the players in Aesop's tales of what to do, and what not to do. Jacen, Jaina, Tenel Ka, Lowbacca, Raynar, Lusa, and Zekk became the next generation of these tales of right and wrong. This is how we learned, and how we grew.

Now, let me say this much. Many are reading this, and seeing a fanaticism in my words, but let me ask you this: is a plant grown in artificial light not still a plant growing? Yes, we knew it was fiction. We knew it wasn't real. We also knew that the Path was right for us, and that the Force had drawn us to these words. Was the Force the same as in these works? For the most part, yes. Was it going to give us telekinesis or the ability to do the Jedi Mind Trick? Not likely, even though we had all hoped it would. This is how we, as a community, developed. We would call out anyone claiming great feats of power, challenging them to perform these skills for the world to see. When they could not, often they were never seen again. Some, however, got passed their ego-driven need to be seen as powerful, and became actual adherents to the Jedi Way.

I even went to the point of writing my own short stories, most of the characters based off of some part of myself that I was having trouble dealing with. They proved to be highly therapeutic, but essentially they ended up being stories of failure. I suffer from a undiagnosed-at-the-time case of bipolar disorder, and many of my more negative emotions were quite a bit stronger than my early-teen control. These stories helped a great deal by allowing myself to live out my fears and feelings of rejection, hopefully to my better end. It was going better than I ever expected it would.

《》《》《》《》《》

THE FIRE OF YOUTH

Then, one fateful day came, and Baal announced he was opening a position within the faculty of the Academy, a lecturer and counselor. I was one of the several who applied for this position, writing the greatest lesson I knew, and I sent Baal this piece of myself, hoping to take the steps forward to becoming a Jedi Knight, to teach the Jedi Way. Well, it did not happen. The position was given to a friend of Baal's named Deean Kett. In hindsight, I was nowhere near ready to shoulder the responsibility of teaching, but I also see that it would have been better the position never been filled.

Deean Kett brought a wave of new information to the Academy, a new life and evolution. He was personable, and very well received. I even liked him, even though his existence grated on my young, jilted ego. He had got my position, and I hated both him and Baal for it. Even though, Deean was a good person that, hate him or not, you couldn't help but like. The man had charisma, I will give him that. He encouraged us to write out a fantasy of how we would deal with situations that he would put forward. Role-playing was, at that early point, still very much accepted as a teaching tool. This helped a great many of them, and I cannot claim to be one who did not partake of this new form of expression. However, it was beginning to get out of control. The website, our Academy, was falling by the wayside, because we were all stuck in the playground all day.

I had reached my limit watching the Jedi I was trying to emulate become nothing more than stage magicians, showing you one thing to wow you out of seeing what was underneath. I broke from the Academy, and began my own Jedi School.

I had a little experience building webpages already, building one for my gamer clan in *Jedi Knight*. I also learned enough about reading through .html script to take the pieces and coding I did not know at that point. So, I built my school, along with other Jedi fed up with the current angle of Deean's teachings: my good friend Jonathan, Josh Steffan, Trad Davin, and Jordan Daeloth. We formed the Jedi of the New Millenium. Yes, it was spelled wrong, and that did not change for a long time. The site was often referred to as JNM or JotNM.

JotNM was filled with people quickly, because I made it the only school at the time to keep an active student roster. This was a school that one could enroll in, and stake their claim to a part of their development. I took several lessons of Kharis's, the man I still call my first teacher, a few of Baal's, a lesson or two from another Jedi school I never had much interaction with, the Force Academy, and the lesson I submitted to Baal in my attempt to make faculty at the Academy. Soon, I had a rather large, if not undeveloped, knowledge base. We had a forum, but it was not the focus of the school. The focus, my focus, was on teaching. I took on the title of Jedi Teacher, and a year later Master. As you can likely see, JotNM was born of my ego, and served more to feed that part of me than to actually help me. As it turned out, Baal was right. I wasn't ready to teach, not that it stopped me.

Somewhere along the way, likely during my reading of the various novels, I got the idea that in order for the Light Jedi to be strong, there needed to be Dark Jedi with which to match wits. The temptation was needed. So, I approached several of the Academy's dark Jedi, asking if they wanted to teach at a sister-school, housed in the walls of JotNM. After being rejected several times, I decided that if they would not follow their path, I would run it, too. I took an alias, and began instructing at Children of the Dark Side, or CotDS. The cover was that my alias had been a local student of mine while I trained with Kharis, before the Jedi had communication. The student fell, and left town for a time. After a while, he had returned, and in an attempt to bring him back, I had offered my alias this school, a shadow in a field of light, hopeful that the interaction with those of the Light would help him to reform.

It was all total crap. I can tell you that I started it because I wanted to help those of the dark come into the light, so my ruse was necessary, but that is a load of crap, too. I was driven to teach, and I wanted my clan of Jedi to be strong, so I put on a mask to bring about their best opponents.

As I am sure you can tell, I was slipping. My Dad had started getting physically abusive, and I was growing more and more angry. I tried and tried, leaning on my Jedi training, to not hate him. To understand what drove him to this. He treated me like a slave in the house. I did all cooking, all cleaning except for laundry. I remember one month in the summer he made me paint the hallways outside his bedroom five different times. When it was all said and done, it ended up the same color it had started out being. To this day, that month confuses me greatly. So, my pressures at home bled over into my training, and caused a great deal more turmoil than I could handle. I hated him for it all.

After a while, I wasn't sure which version of me was the mask, the Jedi or the Darksider. I started a clandestine group within JotNM I called the Guardians, a select group that were let in on the ruse. Of course, I spouted some lie about helping all involved. The point of the Guardians was to help me stay in the Light. They knew of my double roll so they could be my checks and balances. It helped for a time, especially when they became more active in aiding me. One of the Guardians named Kanen proposed that, to help my ruse, he would take it on in kind, becoming the one known as the Master's Will. We built up the clash on the forums for quite some time, the other Guardians objecting to the violence in open forum, all the time knowing the design they were shown.

It was such a great story. A duel between Kanen and my dark alias, where Kanen fell from his path of light into a dark pit of fear and service. The Master's Will an epic tale of the fallen hero. Only in the end did I see what damage was done.

Things stabilized a little until I inducted one other person into the Guardians, Kerian Ambrai. Kerian and I shared a lot of the same influences in our training. He started at Kharis's Praxeum, and had joined the Force Academy, rather than Baal's school, until he became bothered by the constant role-playing that was putting the development on a website, rather than in the person. Young and arrogant as we both were, we had noble enough intentions in our training. Anyway, Kerian's induction caused a lot of waves because I just did it, rather than asking everyone else. I figured I had started the Guardians, and was acting Head of the Guard, why should I have to ask? Yup, arrogant as hell.

As the term of JotNM came to a close, and I was undercutting my alias and reforming those in the dark school, finally fulfilling my originally false reasoning for beginning the school, Kanen became a will of his own. He revealed the ruse, as well as the conspiracy behind its maintenance. Kanen had left the path of the light, and while becoming the Master's Will, he truly began to fill the role. He was a massive irritant for years after that. I still feel bad that he put himself in that position just to help me.

In the digital walls of a school my ego drove me to create, I was betrayed. I handed over control of JotNM to a friend whom I had reformed from his darkness, Juim Teel, and left the Jedi for the first time, burned and angry. Rage boiled in me, because my plan had not been allowed to play out. My dark alias was meant to leave, and those left would either see the error of the dark path, or would leave. That part happened. Several left, seeing the level of deception the darkness could bring. Some turned from their darkness, as Juim had, and struggled to regain balance. Mostly, though, they just left. The difference was that I was no longer trusted in JotNM either.

Kanen had single-handedly destroyed years of what I felt was good work done for a noble cause. Yeah, that was my ego talking. To the ego, one can do no wrong. It didn't matter, though. We had all come to the decision to phase out CotDS, and Kanen had undone it all. My life may have been a great deal different if he had just allowed me to play out the game, and keep JotNM alive. But, no matter how much I might have wanted it, that did not happen. So, for the first time, I left the Jedi.

Jedi Lesson 1

"Life is a paradox in a mystery inside of a puzzle in the paradox of life."

Many future Jedi are first mislead in the beginning of their self-training, which is what is done here at the Academy, by the seemingly simple concept of the nature of the Force...what could be the answer to this puzzling paradox? Some interpret it to be the unyielding, eternal energy of life itself, seeking in a vain, endless search to draw the energy from within when they attempt to use the Force. This it is not. Others believe it to be some sort of omnipotent consciousness, an all-knowing God. It is not this either. And yet others view it as split pair of exact, totally opposite "split halves"...a pair of metaphorical beings, one Yin and one Yang. They see two different Forces, one Dark and evil, the other Light and good. They see these Forces as engaged in a never-ending battle for dominance; this is not the nature of the Force either.

The Force, most simply put, is an ever-growing energy field created, maintained, and enlarged by all living beings. It surrounds us, binds us, penetrates us. It holds the entire universe together. It is neither good nor evil, having no actual Light and Dark Sides. If it did, life itself would be more interesting at the least, but can be put to use for both good and evil purposes. The Force is not an all-aware, all-knowing consciousness, but all the knowledge in the universe can be found within its boundaries. The past, the present, and even many different forms of what will be the future can be found through the enlightenment of the Force.

The Force is best described as a hypodermic needle. With it, the Light Jedi delivers a much-needed medicine. However, the Dark Jedi delivers their deadly, evil poison through this metaphorical needle. Both use indistinguishable means to arrive at totally opposite ends. The Light Jedi uses it while calm and collected, passive; giving them all abilities needed to handle any situation that may arise. Conversely, the Dark Jedi allows their anger to flow through themselves and thus uses the needle while agitated, yielding devastating and destructive results.

It is not uncommon to see a Jedi who can read minds claim they have what is known to be called telepathy. Nor is rare to find a Jedi with clairvoyance gained through the Force that claim they are gifted, or psychic. The Jedi who can bend a spoon with only the use of the Force claims they are telekinetic. In fact, they are none of these. However, some may do it with the Force...and not know it.

Any action in the universe resonates throughout the universe as ripples in the Force. The so-called "telepathic" Jedi can read these ripple and understand what is going on inside of the person's mind. It is not a matter of literally "this ripple means this", but the Force conveys the thoughts and feelings of the person to the Jedi. The very good Jedi mind reader can pick out individual names, numbers, and dates from a person's aura, which is a very hard task. This is a skill that comes with time and practice. If someone has ever given you "the creeps" for one reason or another, that was simply the Force conveying your aura to the other. Oftentimes those feelings are deftly accurate.

Now for those Jedi who claim to be "psychic". Time exists as such: Visualize yourself as Earth itself. The past merely exists as light and sound waves traveling away from the Earth, whereas the future exists as light and sound waves traveling towards the Earth. A clairvoyant Jedi can read these ripples in similar ways as the mind-reading Jedi does. This is not to say that one Jedi cannot be both clairvoyant and a mind reader, it is just putting down the difference. A Jedi can acquire as many skills as one learns.

Finally, the telekinetic "spoon-bender". It is not unheard of for people to bend spoons with the sheer power of their mind and their willpower; these people are called telekinetics. The Jedi, on the other hand, uses other means to perform such feats. The single largest misconception among new Jedi trainees is that the power to move objects comes from within, from the mind. No, this is not true. The power to move objects comes from the Force that is both inside and outside of the body and mind. The mind is merely the means by which the Force is manipulated, the outlet by which a Jedi uses the Force. A clearer mind makes for easier manipulation of the Force. Thus, the Jedi need not possess extraordinary power of mind nor will...merely that needed to use the Force.

Lesson 2: Emotional Control

"Control, control, you must learn control."--Jedi Master Yoda

The Force thrives on balance. The conflicts between the Light and Dark Jedi are as a chemical reaction—they try to reach balance through reaction. Ideally, the Force has an equal balance of Light and Dark, white and black, yin and yang. One cannot exist without the other.

Some Light Jedi see their mission as a purge of the Dark Jedi. They say that they would gladly strike down and Dark Jedi they come across. This is not the way of the Light. The Jedi only fights when there is no other alternative. Let us ponder a hypothetical situation. A Light Jedi was walking down the street when he sees a known Dark Jedi in mortal danger. What does the Jedi do? Do they let their enemy perish and thus eliminate a threat to life? Or do they save their enemy and risk allowing the Dark Jedi to run free and take more life? The Jedi code is to preserve all life. The Jedi is not judge, jury, and executioner. One must respect the Dark and learn from it.

So how does the Light Jedi treat the Dark? As an equal but an opposite. Then what is the difference between a Dark Jedi and a Light Jedi? The Dark Jedi took the easy route to power. Nobody decides to be a Dark Jedi because they wish to destroy and maim and kill. They become a Dark Jedi because it is an easy route to power; a shortcut.

A Dark Jedi is just as human as a Light Jedi. The Dark Jedi merely allows the power to overcome them and they lose control. It is this that leads to destruction and death. Respect the Dark Side, but respect it as you would respect a cobra. Seek to understand it, to find its strengths and weaknesses. But be aware of the harm that can come from it.

Lesson 3: Teamwork

"United we stand...divided we fall."

We as Light Jedi are unique. We are unique in the drive that we have to protect life with the gifts we have been given. We are unique in our techniques: order over chaos, tranquility over entropy. So what? What do these factors that set us apart from all others do for us?

The answer is simple: they unite us. Light Jedi by their nature are a group, a common body. It is important to understand your fellows that you might better understand the common goal you all strive for. While the Dark Jedi try their best to climb over each other to get to the top, the Light Jedi come together and build a stairway. This is your greatest asset; do not underestimate it.

With such a team comes the need for trust. Light Jedi are also unique in that they are trustworthy. You can believe them, confide in them. Do so. For those that worry about their giving the secrets to the Dark Side if they fall, remember this. The fact that you confide in your fellows only ties the common together; trust is the binding fabric of the team.

Never forget these lessons.

Lesson 4: Patience

Patience is a virtue all Jedi should learn; I cannot stress this enough. It is one of the first things you will learn, and one of the most important. If a Jedi is not patient, with his studies and with others, then the pull of the Dark Side increases. You want things quicker and easier, which is the way of the Dark Side.

Many a Jedi have fallen because they believe that their Master is not teaching them as much as they need. They believe they are ready for more knowledge and tests, when in reality they forsake the most important lessons. You must work diligently on the lessons your Master gives you. Explore, learn, and discover every facet of the lesson; master it. Continue to do this through- out your training. You will be presented with more lessons as the time presents itself.

A Jedi must also be patient with others. Let us use an example: You are on a basketball, or football team. The coach is giving you a new play. It seems simple to you; you quickly learn it and perform it well.

There is another player on the team who cannot get it. Every time you run through the play he makes a mistake- he just cannot seem to learn it. Now, you have a choice. You may choose to be angry with him and yell at him for not getting it right. Or, you may be patient with him, and try to help him understand it. I suggest you choose the latter. This way he'll probably understand it, you won't be angry, and you will have learned patience. Not to mention that the play will probably work better.

You see, if you are patient with others, they will have a higher respect for you and a better opinion of you. You will have more friends, and strong friendships. You will also see things from their point of view, and you can benefit others. They can also help you on troubles you have. This begins to teach other virtues: Unity and teamwork.

Be patient in every thing you do. If you watch the Jedi in the Star Wars movies, you will notice that while they might start out reckless (i.e. young Obi-Wan and Luke in ESB), they eventually learn patience. They are coolheaded and able to think clearly in dangerous situations. This is always a plus. So learn patience, practice it, and test yourself in real-life situations. Remind yourself to be patient always. This is the way of the Light Side, and of a true Jedi.

Lesson 5: ...To fall prey to the Dark Side

The Jedi are the defenders of life. In turn, they are the protectors of the Force, for life spawned the Force. The Jedi use the Force to defend life, as well as use the Force to defend the Force. A Jedi must hold the most serious mind, the strongest will, and the undying will to help all living things. All Jedi have an obligation to both themselves and all life on Earth.

The Jedi must also put their heart and soul into everything they do, or they are not true Jedi. A true Jedi worries not with titles, levels of training, or the advancement of their peers. They must worry only of their training. I will explain...

An apprentice or Padawan Learner will eventually earn the title of Knight. But, one of the most important things an apprentice or Padawan Learner MUST learn is that titles are of no concern. When one becomes so obsessed with their title, they tend to exaggerate it, and loose their humbleness. To do that is to fall prey to the Dark Side.

The level of training that an apprentice or Padawan Learner receives is the level they require in the eyes of their teacher. If they have no teacher, then they should not be learning. Although, some do, and they do not realize they progress too quickly, that is when they fall prey to the Dark Side.

If one of your peers advances faster then you in some area of the Force, or even all areas, you should not rush your training to the point you loose yourself in envy of your peers. IF your peers advance faster then you, do not worry, they may have more talent in the particular fields in which they excel. If you loose yourself in envy and eventually, hate, of your peers, you fall prey to the Dark Side.

When I say worry only on their training, I mean worry not about trivial things until which time you are skilled enough to do so. When you choose to leave your training to do something you are not ready for, you loose the advantage of ability, and you run into problems you cannot handle. When you do that, you inadvertently look for easier ways of doing things. To do this is, also, to fall prey to the Dark Side.

Lesson 6: Strength in the Force

A Jedi's greatest asset is the Force. As a Jedi strengthens in the Force, he begins to abandon his constant reliance on his mind and flesh, and instead stretches out with his feelings, turning his attention to the Force. Great Jedi Masters such as Yoda and Obi-Wan were able to sense things 10 feet away or 1,000 light years away.

"I've felt a great disturbance in the Force... as if a million voices cried out...and were suddenly silenced" –Obi Wan Kenobi
They obtained their knowledge not from just themselves, but the energy of life itself. The Force controls your actions, but it also obeys you commands, and as you become more adept in the ways of the Force, you will strike a balance with it. The source of strength for the Jedi also comes from his knowledge and wisdom. Anakin had 20,000 Midi-Chlorians... higher than even Master Yoda himself, yet did this make him a better Jedi than our little green alien friend? I beg to differ!

"Remember... a Jedi's strength *flows* from the Force" –Kenobi

Dark Jedi, however, manipulators of the Force for their own gains, seek only to control others. They believe the order of the universe belongs to them, and care nothing for the natural order of it. Dark Jedi have no balance with the Force, because the dark side controls them... they are slaves to it. Don't be quick to think that Dark Jedi are not clever and shrewd, however... the Emperor was a master manipulator, bending Luke's will until he was almost a lightsaber swing from turning to the Dark side. The Dark side will surely rise like a tide to test your Knighthood, keep your thoughts on the Force, mind what you have learned, and remember, you are never alone.

"The Force is my ally..." – Yoda
"Yoda will always be with you" – Kenobi

Lesson 7: A Jedi's Focus
By: The Late Jedi Ogion,
"May he rest in the peace of the Force"

"Don't center on your anxiety, Obi-Wan. Keep your concentration here and now where it belongs." -- Jedi Master Qui-Gon Jinn

To be anxious is to be worried about some uncertain event or matter. It is not unnatural for a person to become anxious over the future, and it is easy to become overly anxious about the future, as it is always in motion and difficult to see. It is also a simple matter to become anxious about the Dark Side, since its paths are clouded from our view. However, anxiety over the future or the Dark Side (and those who follow its paths) is easily converted into fear. Fear is the beginning of the path to the Dark Side. Fear leads to anger, anger leads to hate, hate leads to suffering.

"Master Yoda says I should be mindful of the future." -- Obi-Wan Kenobi

At the same time, a Jedi must always remember that the actions he takes in the here and now will affect the future, perhaps drastically altering it. A Jedi must carefully consider all possible outcomes of whatever action he takes. While others blunder through life without contemplating the Will of the Force, a Jedi must always be mindful of this, and act so that its purposes are fulfilled.

"But not at the expense of the moment. Be mindful of the living Force, my young Padawan." -- Jedi Master Qui-Gon Jinn

A Jedi must not spend so much time meditating on potential outcomes and possible futures that he loses sight of why he is making the choice. Too much time spent contemplating what could be will cause the Jedi to miss an opportunity to act. And to not act is sometimes worse than to act wrongly.

"May the Force be with you, now and forever." -- Jedi Ogion

《》《》《》《》《》

THE PATH TO POWER

This all happened just about three or four months after I had begun training in the martial arts seriously. I had found an Okinawan Karate teacher at a local community center, and found the next step of my training. I learned to temper my growing aggression towards my Dad by feeding it into my karate. I was angry, and now I had the ability to be strong as well. I let go of the Jedi ideal of emotional removal, and fed everything into my karate training. The Force was no exception. I hated the Jedi that had burned and shunned me, but I knew the Force was with me, so I began to study the energetic systems of various martial arts. At the time, the *Dragonball* Series was just getting popular here in the United States. My experience with the Jedi taught me that inspiration could be found anywhere, so I began to find inspiration in a character of that anime series. His name, Vegeta. His character was born to pride, and he was constantly overcome by the son of a commoner of their race. He was furious, arrogant, and fierce. He was my master, now.

Kerian, whom I believe was just going by the name Ambrai at this point, had broken from the Jedi as well, and was following me tit-for-tat on this path of self destruction. We traded ideas, and martial arts training methods. He was doing some form of American Karate, and we argued often about the value of free-expression versus the traditionalist point of view. One day, for no real reason that I know of, Ambrai just disappeared. It would be some time before I heard from him again.

With all my friends lost to me, and Ambrai just disappearing, I had no reason to stay actively on the internet, so I filled my time with my karate training. I trained so hard and so long, my boxing bag tore down the ceiling in three rooms in the house, and shook the floor and walls of the one above my room when it was there. This solid sand bag became so soft I tore a hole in it one day with a well-placed knife-hand strike. I rocked it so many time with stout knee kicks that the S-hook that held it to the eye-bolt in the ceiling straightened one day, sending the bag crashing to the floor.

I howled and raged, not caring what it made of my character until one day, the abuse stopped. Years and years of fuel all ended that day. The next month, Dad tried to take his aggressions out on my younger brother. That was the first door I ever kicked in, and the first time I ever threatened to kill a man, ready to do so if need be. I had found my power, and refused through gritted teeth, to ever let it go. I was spiraling down a tunnel of rage and pain, unwilling to allow anyone to stop me. Fighting tooth and nail to go further, get stronger, become meaner.

One day, I remember it well, I sat down to meditate before karate class, and could not find my center. Forty-five minutes of calming breaths and gentle focus, and I still could not release my rage, so that I did not hurt anyone in class. That was the first time I went to class and sat out for the night. My instructor never knew of my abuse at home, but by this point, it was gone. He could still tell I was not okay, and he left the class to his assistant, and we went to talk. I remember admitting the rage and hatred. I remember telling how my own father could kick me down the stairs. I remember crying, and nearly punching this man who wanted nothing but to help when he tried to comfort me.

I also remember stopping my rage-training, and taking down my boxing bag for a long time. I had to find my center, or I was going to hurt someone badly for no reason, possibly even kill someone. Yeah, it was that bad. I remember going home long before class ended, ashamed that I had less control at that point than ever before.

I fought my inner demons for weeks after that. There was no end in sight of the darkness that had enveloped me. I fought back to a precarious sense of control. Not balance yet, just control. That control was tested time and again in the fires of my karate training. I was still angry, I was still bitter, but I wasn't sadistic when working with others, and I was forging myself into a living weapon. The fires in my heart helped me to train away my many imperfections. I became an example in class, and often my instructors primary demonstration aid. I was a zealot in my training, and began to enforce upon myself the rigid code of Bushido, the code of the samurai. I also became enchanted by the Eight Poems of the Fist, eight esoteric principles taken from a Chinese text called the *Bubishi*. It is said all the great masters of karate had studied it, and so, I did, too.

I no longer experimented with the Force as I once did. I just trained until it extended with every strike, shielded damage to every defense, and roared like a dragon with every kiai. I remember the surprised look on my instructor's face the first time I overpowered an entire room of people with my kiai. I was proud of that look. It made everything I was doing, all the darkness still hooked to my soul, acceptable. It made it okay. Warriors were supposed to be fierce, Warriors were supposed to have controlled rage, and I was making myself a Warrior. I trained every day, focusing less on my ferocity, I had plenty of that already. Instead, I trained my technique, working kata tirelessly. Years of training, all a blur of "I have to do it again, or I'll never master it".

The hourglass stance of Okinawan Karate is called *sanchin dachi*, named for the old Chinese kata which utilizes that stance exclusively. It is insanely stable, and when you learn to spread your toes as you would your fingers, and grip the floor, it is nearly impossible to break. My instructor and his assistant had devised a test for the stance. They would wrap their belts around the ankles of a demonstrator and try to pull their feet apart, then swap belts, and attempt to pull them together. I loved this test, because it allowed my ego to show off. I would ground my energy into the floor, and the only movement was the two pulling themselves closer to me as they slid on the floor. Well, my foot moved once, and the other foot bled for it. My toes gripped so hard that I pulled up a tile in the room we worked in at the community center. It was an old tile, and they came up often enough, but that mattered little to me. My stance pulled up the floor, that's all I cared about.

I remember when I started helping teach the kids class, I was a purple belt at that point, and was asked to help my instructor because he had just had surgery on his neck. I hated teaching the unruly little imps. Now, don't get me wrong, I love kids. I just didn't like the amount we had to water down the techniques and kata in order to teach young kids. That, and most of these kids were in class because their parents couldn't find a way to tame their abundance of energy. One night, I remember finding a way to tone the kids down some before class, and train at the same time. I would have them all get in a line and make front kicks at me. I would do a low scooping block, grab their kicking foot and the back of their gi and ease them to the floor smoothly. They laughed, I stretched out, they loved it, and I got better at deflecting kicks. It worked very well. We did this at the beginning of the kids class for weeks, and those were some of the best classes because it wore down their initial charge from being at karate class. They were attentive, and got into the class, rather than fidgeting and looking around for something to do. My instructor thanked me for the initiative. That was to be the foundation to the flaring of my resentment.

A month or two into this practice, my instructor decided to hold a sparring class for the adults. It was an awesome night. I sparred against everyone, no matter rank. I was playing to the ability of the student, and had free reign to correct as I saw fit during the match. I was just ever-so-slightly outside of their ability, and pushed them to reach beyond the norm. It wheeled from one student to the next, to my instructor's daughter whom I had a major crush on, all the way to the man himself, my instructor. I was winded from sparring all night, and didn't want to spar him. He was better than me, but I guess it was my turn to reach past my norm. I would always fall for his front kicks. He was a small person, with real short limbs, so he could kick me from my punching range, and I'd never see hem coming. He was a slippery man, even with the forest of hair on his arms.

Well, this match went as expected. I got hit more than I landed, and my instructor moved in for the kill, so to speak. That front kick I always fell for came out fast as a bullet... and just like in the kids class, I scooped the kick and picked the foot up. My instructor, mere months after neck surgery, slammed to the ground with a boom loud enough to make the blood run cold. I remember feeling sick at my stomach, thinking I might have crippled him, or worse. I loved him like a father, then. I remember stepping back in fear, while his daughter ran up to him, about to cry. We were probably the only two in the room who knew how dangerous what had just happened really was. He got up, dusted himself off, shook my hand, and told me he was okay. We laughed about it all night, and he turned it into a lesson for the class that no one is perfect.

The next week, mere moments into my warm-up with the kids, my instructor, so proud of me days before, made me stop having the kids kick at me. It made me wonder, after the high praise for the initiative, then the obvious affect it had on my assimilation of the technique I was using, why would I stop? Then, much to my dismay and eventual disgust, I figured it out. I had hurt his pride. This instance was the first chip of the reason you will never hear me call him my Sensei. He had smiled at me one day, then put his boot on my throat the next. I felt it wasn't fair, and even without my ego screaming bloody murder about, I still feel it isn't fair. However, fair is not how life is.

Well, my distrust eased slightly, and then came the greatest test I had faced in my life up to that point. My instructor took me to Van Buren, Arkansas to the dojo of our regional director, for my Level 1 brown belt test. Remember how I had said I was the chubby kid in school? It turns out my family has a history of hypothyroidism, which means I still carry a good bit of weight. This went against everything our regional director expected of a student of karate. He just thought I was using it as an excuse. So, to prove himself right, he decided this was going to be a very harsh test indeed.

Middle of August, about one hundred degrees outside, in a dojo with a metal roof, freshly re-varnished floors, and no air conditioning. That meant the varnish never dried, making the side of the floor I got put on like walking on super glue. This test is a heated blur for the most part, but I remember feeling the skin tear off my left big toe three counts before it tore off my right big toe. The test was almost over, all I had left was push-ups and sparring. The proper way to do a push-up is to do them with only your big toes touching the ground. The same big toes that were ragged, seeping, bloody pieces of meat at this point. I got through about half of them before I couldn't move anymore from the pain. I just sat up, knelt in the traditional posture, placed my hands on my thighs, and waited.

Our regional director came over to me, smile on his face from ear to ear, and asked why I didn't finish my push-ups. I could hear the pleasure in his voice. He had broken me. I swung my feet around in front of me to show my bleeding toes. He saw them, then looked up the floor to see bloody smears where I had not taken my feet off the ground when I stepped the whole test. I asked for some gauze, so that I could finish them. He told me not to worry about it, and showed me to the first aid kit. I wrapped my feet and finished the test sparring. It took him a month to finally sign a certificate for that test, because he had so badly hoped I was going to fail. His disdain towards me because of my weight just made victory that much sweeter. There are still blood stains in my sandals from the long drive home, where I bled through my bandages.

I had integrated the Force so much into my martial arts that simply putting on my gi still sends a charge through my nerves. It actually became a problem that is so common to martial artists, I could for a long time, only perform as I did in class while barefoot, wearing my pajamas and heavy belt. That made all my training useless if I ever got in a fight not in the dojo. Being that fights don't usually happen in the dojo, that made for quite an interestingly difficult circumstance. The problem came that when I was in normal clothing, I was just as angry, but my mind had put up a wall that, so long as I was not in my gi, my anger was impotent. But, in class, I was a force to be reckoned with.

It wasn't long after that test that I slipped into *mushin*, the state of no-mind, for the first time while sparring. I still only have a hazy recollection of hearing myself kiai, and a fuzzy sense of hitting a floating rib, then finding my sparring partner lying on the ground gasping for air. My instructor did not believe that I did not do it on purpose, he did not believe I had slipped out of myself. Perhaps he had never experienced *mushin* at that point, and lack of evidence lead to a lack of faith. Maybe he just didn't think I was to that point, yet. I cannot say for sure, one way or the other. Either way, his disbelief in what I had experienced just helped the resentment build towards this prideful little man.

My first degree black belt came and went, and I tested for second degree a year ahead of the normal time frame. After that, I was the senior student, the assistant teacher, the right hand of my instructor. I was twenty, and trained enough to be an instructor in my own right. I personally was not ready for that, though. My home life was sickeningly chaotic, I had just lost a job, and had a good friend die just before my second degree test. Her death weighs on me to this day, so I am sure you can imagine how bad it was a decade ago.

It was at this point I was ushered into a job working security by one of the students in the dojo. I worked unarmed at that point as, being under twenty-one, I was not legally able to work armed. Mind you, the difference between armed and unarmed security in Tennessee meant whether or not you were allowed to carry a firearm. I had many other weapons at my disposal, and I was joining a modern version of the path of the Warrior. I was to defend persons and property at my post. It was to be a great aid in my development as a Warrior, on my path to becoming a modern-day samurai. This is the place where I met a Memphis police officer who went by the nickname Heib.

Heib lived as a true warrior. He would come to my work after-hours some nights and work on Iaido drills in one of the high-ceiling empty rooms. Heib had tried to take Iaido from the only man in town who taught it at the time, a man named Harry. He was not allowed to join the class, though, because he did not own a blunted *iai-to* sword. Instead, Heib bought a live blade *shinken katana*. His outlook was that he did not learn to fire a pistol by using a BB gun, or fight with a baton using a foam covered stick. He said if he was going to learn a weapon, he wanted to learn with that weapon, and if Harry didn't want to teach him, then so be it. It was then that I learned respect for another walker of the Path, something I had always had trouble with. This was a man with an aura about him as thick as smoke, a vibrant spot of life in a world of people that had mere wisps of existence. The adage is that a samurai's sword is his soul, but after meeting Heib, I knew that was wrong. No, this man's soul was his sword. Heib died a year later of cancer, but he did not lament his condition. He lived as if every day was his last.

Just before my nidan test, we gained a new white belt named Roberto. He seemed an odd gentleman at first, and I could not figure out why. One night, I walked into class early and found him standing behind our instructor doing some type of free-flow energetic cleansing. It worked, in principal, very similar to reiki, but it felt like no reiki I had ever experienced before. Well, as it turned out, Roberto was a Level One Reiki Master at the time. We began to talk, and I learned he had been studying one form of energetics or another for most of his life. We talked energetics on and off for the remainder of my time at the dojo. This marked the second practitioner I gained a great respect for, so I guess I was getting better. He and I still talk from time to time.

The last straw came just after my instructor's birthday. I had taken up a class collection to purchase him the one thing he said he wanted for his birthday, a functional battle grade katana. He had several wall-hanger swords, but wanted something to place by itself on a stand with pride, a weapon he had no training in, and no experience with at all. I held my opinions on that, but nevertheless, I did as he asked. It had been paid for, and the US Customs drag after the tragedy of 9/11 had dead-locked the sword in port for three months. I told him what the company I had ordered the sword from had been telling me. It wasn't any fault of theirs, things happen. Doubting as ever, my instructor accused me of lying to everyone and just keeping the money. That was a major blow, being that I was contributor of eighty percent of the purchase. He did this standing at the front of the room, just before starting class, in earshot of at least one student. Between that, and my phone being turned off due to non-payment, he said he could not trust me anymore. That had been the largest blow anyone had ever given me in my life. This man I devoted myself to, that I drove around day-after-day because he and his wife shared a car, whose home I practically lived in training at least six hours a day, five days a week, said he couldn't trust me anymore. All over an expensive trinket and a missed phone call.

Two days later, his sword arrived. He did not even try to apologize for what he said. It didn't matter, though. If he had, it would have still been too little, too late. The very next class, I met him in the back changing area, left all the pads and punching shields I had been storing for him, told him where he could stick his precious sword, and left.

Seven Principles of Bushido
Gi: Rectitude
Yuu: Bravery
Jin: Compassion
Rei: Courtesy
Makoto: Sincerity
Chuugi: Loyalty
Meiyo: Honor

BUSHIDO is the "Way of the Military Knight", or the Way of the Warrior. A true Warrior is at all times. These rules are paramount in the Martial Way. They extend beyond the dojo floor, infinitely to all of your existence. The Warrior Path is not a hobby. It is a state of being, and a way of life.

GI: Rectitude
Rectitude means doing the right thing. It is important to always act in the ethical right. This refines your spirit, and makes you a more complete person.

YUU: Bravery
Bravery is standing in the face of injustice, and having the strength to do what is right. It is NOT stepping in where not needed, imposing yourself upon others. Bravery is also standing up for what you believe in.

JIN: Compassion
Compassion has many dimensions. The first of which is the ability to see into a person's situation without bias or prejudice. One must have compassion for the innocent to guard them from injustice. Compassion is also knowing when to not step in, not

allowing them self to become a crutch to those who can stand on their own but won't if no one makes them.

REI: Courtesy

To have courtesy is not always saying what people want to hear, but saying what must be said with respect and dignity. Courtesy is treating others as equals or superiors, no matter their true position, so as to show humility.

MAKOTO: Sincerity

Sincerity and truthfulness go hand-in-hand. Never lie to someone, even to make them feel better. Never misrepresent yourself or those in your charge. Always tell the most complete truth possible, no matter the consequences.

CHUUGI: Loyalty

Never betray those who trust you. Never turn your back on your obligations. Never lie for another person, and never lie about them. Never reveal a hurtful truth to another. Never give out the secrets you're given. This is loyalty.

MEIYO: Honor

Honor is the hardest to know. Honor is not causing a fight, nor is it found in revenge. Honor is not a medallion you show off to those who will listen. Honor is not tales of the past to impress those of the present. Honor is living with discipline, control, and humility. Honor is being Loyal, Sincere, Polite, Compassionate, Brave, and truly Righteous. Honor is NOT face! Often times, in taking a loss of face, an insult, without reaction or retaliation to it, one's Honor grows!

Do you see how each plays a part in the others?

Eight Poems of the Fist
As Taken from the Bubishi

Below are the Eight Precepts of the Bubishi, the Eight Poems of the Fist. These are martial truths that are not immediate. They are, instead, traits that one studying the martial arts should reach for until they are attained. No one of these precepts can be perfected. They are the perpetual quest of every martial arts student.

Below, there will be two meanings for each of these precepts, one looking at life from a spiritual perspective, and the other dealing with martial arts specifically. Also remember, these are not absolute answers. Just as no one precept can be perfected, nor can one be completely explained. This is a guide to understanding, and should be looked upon as a tool to development rather than the epitome of truth.

The Mind is One with Heaven and Earth.

Heaven and Earth are the Supreme Pair. They, together, show the union of all opposites, and how they can both exist at the same time. They are in perfect balance with one another, and are eternal in their place. The Heavens are empty. They represent the Void from which all things come. The Earth is solid and stable, the mass to which we will all return. They exist together, one needing the other. There are many other pairs that follow this same pattern: Life and Death, Over and Under, Left and Right, Inside and Outside, and the most important to the martial artist; War and Peace.

The Mind is One with Heaven and Earth when one trains in the arts of combat, the martial arts, with peace in their mind and harmony in their heart. The martial arts make students more whole. They study the Arts of War to learn the Way of Peace. The Mind becomes immovable: unable to anger, unable to tempt, unable to manipulate. The Mind of a Warrior is the Core of the Universe. No matter how hard someone pushes, they cannot move it.

The Circulatory Rhythm of the Body is similar to the cycle of the Sun and the Moon.

In the light of the Sun, many creatures stir, and by the light of the Moon, they rest. As those creatures settle in for the night, more still creatures rise, being creatures of the dark. Then, as the sun rises, these too rest, and the cycle begins again. So it is with the human body, and the human spirit. As the sun rises, so is the birth of life. It rises, and burns warm. It brings light to the world, as the person matures and grows into an adult. The sun begins to set, as the skills of the person change, and begin to decline. The night falls, and the life wanes, and eventually passes on, ending the cycle. The sun rises again on a new life, and the cycle repeats itself.

This rhythm is like that of the human body. The Sun and Moon are natural cues to the human body as when to sleep, and when to wake. Some work best during daylight, other work better in the dark. The light can be seen as the fresh air we breathe in, giving us the energy to live on. The dark can be seen as the air we breathe out, the toxins of the flesh, trying to pull us closer to our last nightfall. Then, we breathe in again, and the light returns.

The Way of Inhaling and Exhaling is Hardness and Softness.
When one breathes, the body changes from one state to another. Breathing in is the taking in of the essence of life, the air that fuels us. Breathing out is the expulsion of the toxins and waste our body produces. We all know this as the intake of oxygen, and the output of carbon dioxide. However, it goes beyond that. In many meditative practices, the in breath is the bringing in of the energy of life, and the out breath is the pushing away of that which tries to poison our bodies, minds, and spirits. It is seen as breathing in a golden light, and breathing out a putrid black smoke.

In combat, it is seen that these breaths also bring about different states of being within a martial artist. The body is soft when it draws in breath, clinging at the ability to exist. The harder someone is breathing, the more they are clawing at the spark of life within them. When we breathe out, we expel death, if even for an instant. We become hard, resolved to the task of soldiering onward. To a martial artist, this means that we look to strike our opponent when they breathe in, reaching for a breath of life. Also, it shows us when we ourselves are most vulnerable. Always defend ones self when breathing in, or the fate you hold for your opponent, you may share. Strike when breathing out, the increase resolve, but to hit an opponent who is also breathing out will be like hitting a wall with a brick, both sides are damaged.

Act in accordance with Time and Change.
This tenet holds several meanings. It shows us how to live our lives, always remembering that things do change, and we have to

change with them, or we grow stagnant, and wither away. It also shows us we must look back to see the course taken before us, and choose from them which one fits any given situation best.

When locked in a bout for one's life, Time and Change are all the more important. Time refers to the timing of the fight, and of the opponent. Often, an attack is fast, dirty, and over very quickly. We must realize this, and respond to an attack just as quickly. Chance is seen in the change of a person's attitude, tactics, or timing; to offer an advantage over your opponent. Always be mindful of the timing, and the change of that timing.

Techniques will occur in the Absence of Conscious Thought.

A technique, be it in combat or in life, that one has to think about will be slow and useless. We are taught how to read and write from our earliest days of schooling, and as such, when we enter the world in which we need this detailed form of communication, we no longer have to think about what these bent lines mean, we simply see letters and words, sentences and stories.

A combative technique is very much the same in its effect. Any technique one has to think about will be inadequate, and possibly put them in harm's way if ever tested. We train blocks, strikes, stances, and movement so that when such are needed, we do not have to think about all the minor details. The mind will see a threat, and before it can process it, the body will react to that threat, moving you our of distance, or redirecting a strike to a less vital area. If we think too much, in basic training, sparring, or actual combat; all the techniques we learn and know are useless. They are just in the way of our staying safe.

<u>The Feet must Advance and Retreat, Separate and Meet.</u>
If you stand still, you will be run over. You must learn to flow with the rhythm of life, and bend with the winds of life and change. Sometimes you will be stretched thin, others you will excel. At times you will be too crowded to breathe, and others you will have to take a step back. Resolve yourself to the fact that this is part of life, and in time, you will no longer be worried over the outcome of trivial matters.

When fighting, the movement of the feet as just as important. Stand still while someone is striking you, and you are nothing more than a boxing bag that bleeds. You must move, and continue to move. Never stop moving. There is no difference in one more from the next. It is constant flow, never breaking, never stopping. Be it forward in attack, back in deflection, or taking a long step to get out of the way, one must always move. However, do not move so much you are out of control, keep your center as your flow, and you will succeed.

<u>The Eyes do not miss even the Slightest Change.</u>
Many people throughout the world live in a kind of haze that blurs them from the truth of their existence. They shut out what they do not want to see, or accept. They live in ignorance, and that is no way to be. To walk with one's eyes closed is of no good, unless you want to peek out one day and have no ideal where you are.

When locked in combat, you must be ever-vigil in your observation of surroundings. If you are fighting one person, be mindful that they might have friends lurking just out of your tunneled vision. If you are not in a broad open field or empty room, be sure to know where the puddles are, or a chair that you can wither put between you and the aggressor, or use it directly as a weapon itself. If something changes, for instance you enter an area darker than that around you, even before a confrontation, scan the area. Be sure you know where the pipe is next to the dumpster in case you need it.

The Ears listen well in All Directions.

The eyes are not the only sense one needs. Hear what happens in the world around you. Listen at the water cooler at work, watch the news, read the paper. Keep your ear to the ground, and life will seldom surprise you completely.

Always keep your ears open for the signals or an attack. Someone speedily walking your direction, or you hear a chain rattle. The crunch of gravel, the breaking of a bottle, the opening of a knife. These are all unique sounds that can clue you into an attack mere moments before they happen, so that you can prepare to defend yourself, and/or those around you.

Budo: The Key to Peace

In the days of martial warfare, combat was a way of daily life. If you did not know how to fight, you were dead. Plain, and simple. You could easily be walking down the road, and be challenged to a fight-to-the-death. Part of it was the time's violent nature, and another part was the bitter rivalry between schools of combat at that time. That was a sad time for the development of human nature, but it did bring about the development of the martial arts...so some good came of it, at the very least.

Well, today, we are in infinitely more danger than people then were. However, we are not in the same state of constant danger. We can, at times, let our guard down. Not the safest idea on the planet, but it happens sometimes. Well, the question now becomes, why train just as diligently as the masters did when they were in a much more prolonged state of peril than we are?

Well, the martial arts have changed with time. They were *bujutsu*, but are now *budo*. The combative knowledge is still there, but the arts have developed into a way to not only protect one's self, but to purify one's spirit at the same time. We still learn how to defend ourselves from any and all types of attacks we may encounter. We are still armed with an adaptive arsenal of strikes, blocks, kicks, locks, throws, and other various moves to combat any threats we may encounter. However, in the altered state of the martial arts, we are now clear of mind and in enough emotional control to know when to use our fighting skills, and when to not. Not to say that did not happen in the past, but in this day and age, we are more able to rely on our spirit to avoid combat rather than our limbs quickly ending it.

Also, through the meditative states brought on through proper practice of a *budo*, we are able to transcend the rational mind at times, and gain little glimpses of cosmic insight. This knowledge is relative to all mankind, and should be shared. Oftentimes, such understandings cannot be put into words, but can only be relayed through experience. In this, we pass on what we have learned, keeping both the traditions alive, combat and spiritual refinement.

Mindset of a Warrior

The mindset of a warrior calls for a change in perception, without which proper martial spirit cannot be developed. This change of perception cannot be done overnight. It will take constant work to make this change be felt in your being. This change is to differentiate between practice, and training.

The outlook of practice is a dangerous one to a warrior. When one practices a martial art, it requires the practitioner to think about the exact mechanics of a techniques so as to achieve technical proficiency in that movement. Movements are done slower, with less power, or to intentionally exaggerate certain aspects so that one might remember to perform that particular detail when the time comes. Practice in an act of mindful action; a slow and methodical repetition of technical skills. There is a time for such actions, but they are early in one's martial career.

Training, on the other hand, is to be the true outlook of a warrior. While practice is a matter of proficiency, training is a matter of life-and-death. The martial arts are the arts of death. There is no light way to say it. They are serious in their nature and severity, and should not be looked at otherwise. To train, one must hold only the outlook of death. A warrior must feel that if they do a technique incorrectly, they may die from its misuse. Training is not seen as "when the time comes". Training is seen as "I can, and possibly will need this technique this next instant to save my life". There is an urgency to their execution: urgency, but never haste. In fact, practicing a technique can take hours. Training a technique takes a lifetime.

One always trains, be they in action, stationary, or sleeping. A warrior must never stop training. They seem to be obsessive in their pursuit of perfection, but this is not so. They are driven to train, but not obsessed. Obsession implies a lack of control regarding the action they perform. A warrior is the model of self-control, and self-discipline. It is through this control that they are able to undertake the training they are called to do. Those who train do so so that they might never be caught unprepared for anything. So, take this mindset to heart, and feel it in your being.

Train, do not practice!

《》《》《》《》《》

INTO EXILE

After leaving the place I considered home for so many years, I was lost. The path of the Jedi seemed to have yielded nothing, and the path of the Warrior had left me a *ronin*, the term used for displaced samurai. Their master would die, usually in a battle but sometimes in a political plot, and there was a time when the ritual suicide to follow one's master into the next life, *seppuku*, was made illegal. So, these displaced samurai became the Wandering Men. They would, sometimes, be taken up by a different clan who was loyal to their former master, but more often than not, they became bandits, so shamed by their Code's command to follow their master but their inability to do so, that they willingly lost the last shreds of their honor in survival. So, I went back to the refuge of the internet, and spent a great length of time speaking only with a great friend and former Jedi named Joshua.

Josh was, even so many years ago, a brilliantly spiritual person, who had such a poignant way of phrasing things so that even his simple words hit your mind like a sledgehammer. He is no different to this day, thank the Force. He trained in Old Yang style Tai Chi Chuan, and a form of Kung Fu that I cannot remember the name of for the life of me. He was my sole confessor, my greatest critic, and my deepest support. I would not be anywhere near where I am today without his friendship and guidance. It was while speaking with him for all this time that I began to find a sense of balance, and was likely the first time I had felt peace in my entire life. Most night, when we spoke, it is trivial day-to-day things or some martial arts anecdote his teacher had told him. Some days we would speak for hours on end, others, he would say a few short words, and have to leave, busy with home problems of his own.

We spoke often of our distaste for the Jedi Community. After a time, I had forgiven those I felt had burned me, and realized I was the source of most of my problems when I was teaching at JotNM. Josh's story was different. He got burned out with the undercutting and lies from many of those he trusted. He was part of a movement called the Jedi United. It was to be the first makings of an Order, but one of the core group who were building this took the structure, and used it for their own ends, changing little more than the name. That was the way the Jedi Community worked, though. It was far from the enlightened namesake we all claimed to want to be.

One thing that Josh helped me with was understanding the difference between *qi*, the energy of life, *yi*, the energy of the mind, and *jing*, the energy of manifestation. These were all of the Force, but varied differently in their vibration, and what they did. Josh had told me the reason my energetics did not work without being in my gi was because my mind, my *yi*, was not producing *jing* unless my mind was set on the intensity of training. So, running with this idea, I began to study the different forms of energy people claimed to, knowing all were of the Force, but not knowing what they all were. I also began to train by myself, working my way out of my gi, a little at a time. My mind was no longer locked in my gi, and my energetics flowed freely again. My understanding, though, had began to change once more. That's the point, though, isn't it?

From that study came the ZenRyoku Mindset. *Zenryoku* means full circle, and I felt this was the coming of a greater understanding of the Force. The ZenRyoku Mindset broke down all energetics into four major vibration groups. Qi, the energy of the body; Psi, the energy of the mind; Suki, the energy of emotions; Kon, the energetic soul. In hindsight, it was a strange way to view the energetic self, but it is what I needed at the time. I worked on internalizing this outlook, and began to ease myself back into the Jedi to share my revelation with the masses. It didn't last long at all, because I was very much wrong in my outlook. I was still angry, and egotistical. I was still arrogant, and petty. The problem was, instead of explosive fury, I had become condescending. It wasn't bad enough that I was soiling my reputation and taking advantage of the little trust anyone had in me, but I was looking down on them at the same time. How small a person I still was, no matter how much my ego wanted to be a god amongst men, a revolutionary scion to the Path. I tried to take an apprentice in this outlook. No worries, it didn't last.

I even went as far as to try to visually show my resurrection by making a second set of Jedi Robes, one of the quirks I still held onto from when I started. These things were horribly arrogant. Silver and leather, and a huge white outer cloak, complete with embroidered leather cuffs.

My flashy show of artificial devotion didn't work, on others or on myself. I stepped back into the mists, and released it all again. I began to think of myself as a new form of Jedi, and said as such to Josh. He tore into me with the ferocity of a starving pack of wolves. He tore down all the ego-driven bullshit, he likely would have spat on my bright white robes had he been physically present. He told me that the Jedi Path does not bend to the person. It was the job of the individual to bend themselves to the Path. He was saying what, years later I would tell many others: the Path is rigid, but the Way unique. The Path, the philosophical program that molded a Jedi, that was what we strove for. The Way was our unique experience, our successes and failures, of keeping to the Path. Like I said, Josh was good at hitting me with a sledgehammer when he needed to. This was more like a shotgun blast.

I sat down, and wrote the first of my Holocrons, a word taken from *Star Wars* that was used to describe their record-keeping of the Jedi teachings and methods. I didn't do this to prove him wrong, merely to make myself remember this Path that dominated my life. What I wrote was basically a Jedi training manual. My first attempt at this held no real benefit to my problem, but it was a start. It spoke of the theory and theology of the Force, held tenets for becoming a walker of the Path, but it lacked what I lacked, emotional control. Not denial, just control. I cannot say it was not a well-made guide to the Force, but it just was not what I needed then. It was wrong.

This was about the time my second adviser came back to me. His name at the time was Starr. Starr was a direct student of my old Grey Jedi friend, Koren Jey from Baal's Jedi Academy. He had taken over JotNM from Juim Teel several years before, and had eventually changed the name to Temple of the Jedi Arts. The site still held onto the original idea of having an active student roster. Starr and I had crossed paths some weird way that I cannot remember. It just happened, as it was meant to. This is how the Force is. Starr read through my first Holocron, and he asked me why I wrote an advanced text. He mentioned that the work is good for an experienced Jedi, but very few of the beginners would not lose themselves in the pursuit of some of what was written there. He also taught me a very valuable lesson in that we are the Jedi of this existence, not some generations-old space-cult. We have to be willing to not be carbon copies. By this point, Episode II had come and gone, and everyone was trying to assimilate the ways of the Old Republic Jedi. Everyone but me, and Starr. We both agreed that the Order of Old Republic Jedi fell because they were flawed, blinded by their dogma and tradition. He charged me with fixing that in the Jedi Community, whether he meant to or not.

So, I began digging deep in the crates, all the way back to Kharis, Baal, and the early days of JotNM. The untainted view of the Jedi as laid out in our beginning. I knew that in order to save the Jedi, I had to first save myself, and in order to do that, I had to learn control. I started to work on myself during my worst moment, driving. I learned road rage from my Dad, and the longer I lived without control, the worse it got. In an attempt to squash this problem first, I wrote down the Jedi Code, and added lines to it that I had trouble with in my daily life. I took the Code from four lines to seven. I wrote it on a piece of paper, and stuck it on my dash, over my tachometer. Whenever I would feel myself getting too angry, I would take a deep calming breath, glance down at the piece of paper, ease off the gas some, and recite the seven lines of my Code over and over again, always eyes on the road, until I was calm and I had found my center.

Oh, the wondrous work it did. I typed up this Code, and laminated it on a business card, keeping it my pocket at all times. Just as I did with the copy in my car, if I began to lose my temper, I would touch the card in my pocket, remember what I was supposed to be, and recited the lines of the Code until I was calm. I began to explore all my other lessons, as well as Baal's, Kharis's, and several Starr had given me, and found which line or lines of the Code each one applied to. I made it my place to know this Code inside and out. I scoured the internet for other interpretations of the Jedi Code, and found almost as many as I did people within the Community. Some were shallow in their explanation, many were very well thought out, one or two were profound.

Through the study of these Codes, I began to learn to truly control my temper, and let go of my negative emotions as they happened. It was at this point that I began to see the Force as a multifaceted stone, with no true light or dark side, merely a shaped facet interpreted differently by each who viewed it. Gods, energies of another name, emptiness. They were all the Force, depending on the perspective of the one looking. I had become a true Jedi for the first time in my life, and remember fondly the night that my ever-present adviser, Josh, had said as such. Having finally found my feet, I sat down and wrote an entirely new Holocron. This one was geared towards beginners, and to refresh those on the Path who, like myself, had neglected the basics for far too long. I had decided, upon completion of that work, that it was time for me to reinsert myself into the Community.

ZenRyoku Mindset

Life springs not from a singular being, or a collection of all-powerful gods and goddesses. Life springs forth from the harmony of the numerous life energies held in the bounds of this universe. Through a universal fluke, these energies have aligned themselves in such a way as to allow life to begin and carry on. Below is listed the major universal life energies:

Psi– The Energy of the Mind
Ki– The Energy of the Body
Suki– The Energy of the Heart
Kon– The Energy of the Soul

All cultures have assigned numerous labels to these life energies, as well as what was believed to be their boundaries and origins. In some cases, different labels on the same life energy will conflict in one way or another, bringing about the numerous religions on this world. However, one cannot just have one of these energies, because if one were to take one of these energies away, they would fall out of balance, and would cease to exist on this plane, or likely on any other.

A person, any person, has the abilities to control most, if not all, of the life energies. Some choose to develop some energies over others. For example, a Psionics practitioner may not to choose to develop all of their abilities in ki, if they choose to develop any. A ki warrior might decide no to develop their suki. That is a very poor outlook on life. Each sect of energy user believes the path to ultimate perfection is through sticking to one energy style, when in fact, one must develop all energies of life to be truly mastered in their energy work. A developer of kon has an advantage over most of the other energy users, though. Kon is not an energy that is used directly, but rather assists in the development and control of the other life energies.

Example:
One would not use kon to heal a person, but instead would use their kon to help control their ki and suki, the energies used when healing. The ki would heal the physical damage to an extent, and the suki would restore the energy of the heart to the injured.

Psi- The Energy of the Mind

Psychic abilities have been reported in a number of fashions, such as telepathy, empathy, and telekinesis. All these are abilities the mind can develop, as well as many, MANY more. Scientific studies show that human beings, in our current state of evolution, only use around 10% of our brain actively. However, through discipline and time, one can increase that to as much as 50%-60% by undertaking a serious psionic training regiment. However, everyone on the planet uses their psychic abilities everyday. Simple thought, no matter how unimportant; reflexes; and all forms of memory...all are typical psychic abilities inherent in most all of the human race.

Ki- The Energy of the Body

The work Ki is Japanese for life or spirit, and is an energy centered in the human body. Its Chinese equivalent, chi, also means spirit. The Chinese state that chi cannot be left in the human brain, or the energy becomes stagnant and is a poison for the mind. This is due to it interrupting the flow of psi. This shows the level of interaction of the life energies. Ki development can do a multitude of things: speed up physical movement, release/reduce physical stress, and increase physical endurance as well as build up a strong shield against physical illnesses, as well as many more things. However, one must notice something in all those listed examples, the word shared there is physical. This is due to the fact that ki holds no control over the emotions, but rather their control over the human body. Ki poisons the human brain, therefore damaging the flow of a human being's psi.

Suki– The Energy of the Heart

Suki is Japanese for love, the one true energy linked in the human psyche to the heart, but never on such a mystical level. When it is said, energy of the heart, it is not meant as the energy that flows through the actual organ, for that energy is ki, the energy of the body. Suki more refers to the energy brought on by different emotional states. There can be both positive and negative suki. Positive suki would be from joy and love, whereas negative suki would be from depression and hatred. Suki can diminish ones ki to the point that is brings on illness. Intense negative suki, such as anger or loathing, may increase the blood flow, therefore increase the ki flow in the body. Love and euphoria can do this as well. However, positive suki and negative suki can also slow the flow of ki through the body. Contentment, positive suki, would slow the energy flow down; as would depression, negative suki.

Kon– Energy of the Soul

Kon literally means soul. This is an energy developed by few in the energy working communities and cultures. It holds a degree of control over the other life energies. By such, it is meant that by using Kon, it makes it easier to control the other life energies.

I refer back to my example of the healer. If one were to try and use their ki and suki at different times, they may break the precious balance of the internal energies. Kind of like taking a hanging scale and putting 3 marbles on one side and none on the other. It tips to one side. Well, after is settles like that, say one puts three marbles on the other side as well. The scales move erratically for a god amount of time, and eventually settle. However, the turmoil caused by doing it one piece at a time might have done more damage then good, and the energy user would have no idea until it was far too late to do anything about it. Through development of kon, the energy user would have allowed themselves to put a marble on each side of the scale at the same time, therefore maintaining balance.

《》《》《》《》《》

OUT OF THE MISTS

I had received a message from a former colleague of Josh, asking me if I wanted to take the position of head administrator in the online training program he was beginning. I respectfully declined the position, instead taking the offer of vice-principal of philosophical studies, head of Force studies, and overseer of the Solo Training program, that made use of my training manuals. This man's name was Relan Volkum, and his site was called JEDI. JEDI was the home of the Jedi Realist movement, something done to save us all from the role-playing history we all shared. Not all Jedi were Realists, but most were. I was not, totally. They tried to take too much of the mystery out of the Path. They were removing the faith-based aspects of it all. They treated the Force as a tool, not as something beyond themselves.

Relan was a quiet, peaceful person. He had a grand plan for the Jedi Community, and because of the quality of his design, both in social interaction and in the development of his students, JEDI quickly became an epicenter for the Community at large. His ambitions were lofty, but his planning was detailed, and his patience knew no ends that

I had ever seen. I was honored to be a part of those plans, and that time.

Relan and I spent years discussing the direction the Jedi were taking, and the ever-growing problem of ego-driven in-fighting, and those who did not think they had to fit themselves to the Path. I was not alone in that respect, it would seem. JEDI seemed to be everything Relan had wanted it to be. The training program was well-staffed, and well-maintained. There was the standard group-learning Academy Path, the Solo Path that I was in charge of, and the Traditionalist Path of one-on-one apprentice learning. There were always far more would-be apprentices than would-be teachers. That was perhaps the only failure of the entire program, and it still did well enough. Force studies was easy enough to do. Assignments were given, with a certain amount of leeway on outcome. I often spoke of my history, and gave technique experiments to the more advanced students. Guest- and student-lecturers were welcome, and often. Starr made several appearances in the digital halls of JEDI, but I never could get Josh to come in. I would later find out that JEDI was the old Jedi United program, and it was actually Relan who had taken the work and ran with it. Josh was no longer upset by it, and when I confronted Relan about it, he seemed very shamed by what he had done. I could not judge someone for their ego-driven mistakes, as many as I had made.

I loved running the Solo program, because I always felt that students who came into their own understanding were the most stable. The were moments of revelation, not a lesson on some computer screen. It was a far more intimate level of understanding, and was a lot harder to shake. They would report on their progress, and those who asked for it, received my Training Manuals to supplement their learning experience. Many times, they would disagree with part of the Manual, and a debate, a civil debate which was so rare on the forums those days, would ensue. We would discuss points and counter-points, and when all perspectives were shown, I often found most of the misunderstanding was because the person had skipped something earlier in the text. It was one of the Solo students that first referred to me as "Master" to someone else. I didn't think I deserved it then, but Relan agreed with the student, and changed my subtitle on my account to "Master Jedi". By that point, even Josh agreed I deserved the recognition, and he said my denial of being worthy of it was proof that I was to that point. I'm not sure how much I believe that mindset, but I quit arguing it after a few weeks.

As vice-principal over the whole program, I helped Relan to refine many of the problems in his early program as they arose. We worked on more accurate progress-reporting. We set the precedent of strongly recommending the study of a martial system as part of the training, with lengthy explanations why, and even testimonials from several of the students and staff who practiced as to the benefits it had given them. That one surprised me, coming from the steadfast pacifist Relan was. Anyway, we were taking the online training of Jedi into a whole new era of complexity, and it was working. We were repairing the faults of many years of us just not knowing.

After a year or so, I had to leave the internet for a period of about seven months, only able to check in once a month at most. I resigned my positions, and even made recommendations for my replacements in each department. I knew everything would be okay, because

Relan was strong, and JEDI was stronger than both of us. While I was gone, I began to work on a new method of teaching, I called the Temple Method. It was based on the slow personal progression often found in Monastic societies.

I used many of the articles and techniques explained in my Holocrons, but I only revealed them one lesson at a time. I opened a new school site, called Students of the Force. Yes, I like prepositions in my website names, not sure why. As if to simulate a cross between a vow of silence and my early days, I had a roster of 6 students, and no way for them to interact. By this time, so many sites had gone to forum-based learning, and had so little control, I refused even that. The student body was made of some of the shining-stars at JEDI in what was my Solo program. I reworked the lessons, not in content, but in structure. I labeled them in a way that they would mention what aspect of training each exercise covered, and what it built upon. Since my exile, I had become such a staunch believer in the Code being the foundation of all Jedi training, at the bottom of each article and exercise, I listed the 7-line Code, and highlighted the line or lines of the Code it applied to.

After a little longer than my seven month hiatus, I returned to JEDI, just in time to see the election of a Council, something the Jedi Online had been trying to do since the first appearance of the Jedi Council in Episode I. It held a great deal of potential, plucked from the best and brightest at JEDI, but it was also stained with some of the larger egos at JEDI as well. I even heard I was nominated for a seat, but was left off the ballot due to my inactive status. The members of this Council were the logical Nabledan, the charismatic Aslyn, the old-timer Brandel, headstrong and logical Nyara, everyone's common sense Moonshadow, staunchly devoted Arias Mourns, and one of my former Solo program students, a law officer by the name of Faris Najib. This Council wanted to do so much, as we all wanted them to do. The down side to having some inflated egos on such a committee as this was that there was never any chance they would respectfully bow their head to the majority, and subside their own desire for the greater good.

I remember one time, the Councilor Aslyn had been acting very unprofessional in some series of threads, going back to the ego-driven lashing out he had been known for in the past. I brought this to the attention of my long-time friend Brandel, and the Council Head Seat, Nabledan. I said I did not mention it directly to Aslyn, publicly or privately, because I did not want to show any lack of support for this Council. I wanted it to work as much as anyone, maybe more than some of the Councilors. I knew that if I took it to Aslyn directly, he would take it personally, and I felt the conduct of a Councilor was an internal matter. They both thanked me for my concern, and said they would address the problem. They did, but Aslyn brought the fight to me about it. I gave him the same reasons I gave Brandel and Nabledan, and he eventually agreed he was acting out of position. In the end, my support was still to the Council, and Aslyn and I had reached an agreement of a sort.

The Council had moved away from JEDI, onto its own site. It was no longer the Council at JEDI, but now, it was going to try to become the Jedi Council. Nyara, however, still held a teach position at the Academy at JEDI. The Council had asked for anyone who had anything to discuss with the Council to feel free. I remember submitting a proposition I had developed for the foundation of a true, physical Order. A goal, a centralized place of communion. A way to take the message to the world. It was grand, and a long-term view of the possible. Nabledan loved the idea, and Brandel said he had been working on something very similar. Aslyn didn't like the idea, but he saw the benefit. Arias saw problems with the details, but over-all he was okay with it. Faris and Moonshadow reserved themselves for a time, until all ideas and concerns were addressed.

Nyara, on the other hand, she did not like it at all. She went into a faculty-only locked forum on JEDI, and began to vent her frustrations. She said my plan looked fanatical, and power-hungry. She felt I was too close to Nabledan, and was trying to insert myself into the Council. Allow me to dispel that. Nabledan and I had become good friends at this point, kindred spirits who respected one another to the utmost. I *had* expressed to him that if anyone were to leave, and he needed a new seventh member, I was willing to accept a nomination. I stated I would sit on the Council, if the Council needed me. That was all. Back to the point, Nyara attacked two major points in my proposal. She asked questions like *Why study the Force?* and *Why study the martial arts?* The very idea that someone could reach so high in the Community and not know the answers to those simple questions shocked me. I know how the martial arts helped me to tame my inner demons. Without my martial arts background, I would never have had the strength to overcome my darkness during my exile. She even asked *Why learn the Jedi Code?*

I am ashamed to say I lashed out. I was going to let it all go, until the attack against the Code. I had spent years making the Code my life. Nyara was a Jedi Realist to the extreme, and JEDI had grown to accept her point of view. She had many supporters there, and they all agreed. I told them all where I saw their folly, but spent most of the message attacking Nyara's cowardly action. I was no longer on the staff at JEDI, so I should not had still had access to the faculty forum. She was trying to hide this from me, in a place where I was unlikely to find it. After my diatribe, I informed her, step-by-step, how to block me from seeing her continued attacks. Within minutes, she followed those instructions. Nevertheless, I had copied the entire conversation, and informed Relan of the misuse of the Faculty Forum, something merely designed to discuss guest speakers and possible curriculum changed. That was my last day at JEDI, and Relan, already a little unhappy with the direction JEDI's Academy had taken, shut it down shortly thereafter.

Word got out of Nyara's actions, though not from me, and it added to the fuel of the attacks against the Council. It folded shortly thereafter. No one that I know has heard from Nabledan since then.

Jedi Holocron
Jedi Training Guide/Information Source

This is something the Jedi of Earth have been wanting for years now, but to little good. The mass amounts of knowledge the Jedi hold are not easily stored, and could very easily take a lifetime to collect. I have dedicated my life to that feat, and as such will not rest until all the knowledge of the Jedi is stored here.

FYI: In most of this text, the Jedi will be represented from the male perspective. This is not to say that there are no female Jedi, but rather that I did not want to clutter the document with "he/she" and "his/her", making it that much more confusing. I apologize to anyone this may offend, for it was not my intention.

Table of Contents:
-History
-Philosophy
-Mannerism
-Physical / Martial Training
-Techniques

Section One: Jedi History
The Path That Lies Behind Us

The History of the Jedi is a short one, but not the one a person would think of by hearing the word "Jedi". True, the concept of the Jedi came from a George Lucas film phenomenon, but the idea didn't just spring out of the mind of Mr. Lucas. The outlook and mannerism that make up the Jedi way actually came from the Eastern religion of Taoism [Daoism]. Certain aspects of the Jedi philosophy were removed that the true Jedi of Earth have denounced as just plain old wrong. Such things include the outlook of "sides" of the Force. The Jedi of old did not publicly hold this view before they disappeared, or left on their own paths.

Kharis Nightflyer
Father of the Jedi Order

The Jedi Knight known as Kharis Nightflyer was the one considered the father of the Jedi Order for many reasons. He was the first in a group of pioneers in the act of offering the Jedi arts to the public. He was the first to document Jedi techniques, as well as the first to host a small, although efficient training academy. As small as this place was, and as limited its media, it is still the starting point of many Jedi's training. Keeping with the old ways, his teachings quote the useable lines of Alec Guiness and Frank Oz and were laced with the old thoughts of Light and Dark Jedi, and the uprising of the Sith. At this point, all dark Jedi were termed Sith, because it was the only term known to use for such beings of the Force. Jedi Nightflyer was also the first to bring in yoga and qi-gong techniques, changing them so as to make them Jedi in wording, and useful Force skills for any Jedi to know. While Jedi Nightflyer was felt to be the one to begin the training of Jedi, he was rarely ever doing any actual teaching. Instead, Kharis made public his Jedi skills in written form, for all to find and learn from. This left much room for personalization and expansion. As such, it fostered the discovery of countless skills through the Force: some useful, others pointless.

The Jedi Academy
Birthplace of the Jedi Knights

Baal Legato's Jedi Academy was the first large scale training grounds for Jedi Knights. Jedi Legato pioneered the use of a group faculty to teach different areas of the Jedi Arts. The Academy, known more popularly as the JA, held lessons on such things as Jedi Philosophy, Force lessons, Saber Combat lessons, and even discussions on the Dark Side...not *just* condoning its use, but understanding how the Dark Side took hold of a Jedi's being, so that they might avoid such things. It was also the first to adopt the use of message boards to spread the knowledge of the Jedi to others. Through this message system, Jedi Legato's JA spawned the eventual fondness of creating and sharing such texts as are located in the various stores of Jedi Lore. Jedi Legato was a fair man, with a strong sense of compassion to those that he called his "students", although he never said such things aloud. Other great Jedi among the faculty of the JA include Mal'Kith, a dark Jedi of amazing wisdom; Lark Kedder, the saber teacher, teaching Japanese style and spreading the wisdom of the famed swordsman Miyamoto Musashi; and finally Deean Kett, a wise Jedi Philosopher who brought both levity and enlightenment to the establishment. This Academy spawned many of the Jedi that would become the leaders of the Order. During this time, the master-apprentice idea took hold, whereas before nearly all Jedi were self-trained.

Koren Jey
Lord of the Grey Jedi

Lord Koren Jey was the first recognized advocate of the Grey path of the Jedi. Light and Dark Jedi both shunned him for what he was, and yet all respected him for the path he took. At the time, the idea was either you were light or you were dark, and there was no middle-ground. Koren paved the way for the acceptance of the outlook that now dominates the Jedi in the Order. The outlook of the Grey Jedi was that no matter how one went about obtaining their goal, as long as the goal was for the good of another, it was not evil. The ends justifying the means. Lord Jey was not only a great Jedi philosopher, but he was also a great warrior, and eloquent poet. Koren left the Jedi Community to strike out on his own search for purpose.

Enter the Shadow
The Truth of the Force

The Shadow Jedi are by far the single most fateful thing that has happened to the Jedi. They dispelled the outlook of sides to the Force. These new breed of Jedi showed the truth of the Force's neutrality time and again, teaching a lesson to all Jedi. The Force was not a coin, with sides or colors; but rather an energy field, a mass of pure energy that vibrates, and allows all to be. The 'dark side' was not of the Force, but of the Force-user. That which had been ingrained in the Jedi outlook since their birth on this realm, the 'dark side' was a way to rationalize away a person's ability to truly be evil in their heart. The Shadow Knights, distancing themselves from the Jedi, used an outlook spawned from Ninjutsu, and as such their outlook on the Force and their sense of duty towards it are also different...yet startlingly similar. These are the Jedi that have held the truth about the Force for all these years. Slowly, yet surely, the Jedi are coming to realize the truth behind the outlook of the Shadow Jedi...that there is no "dark side". With that outlook will come a new way of understanding the Force, and a new way of training the Jedi.

The Jedi United
Unity Amongst the Ranks

By far the most dramatic step towards one Order of Jedi, a group known as the Jedi United were the first major stepping stone in the unification of the Jedi. At this point, many little cliques had formed within the Order, spreading themselves all over the place. All were teaching the exact same thing, and yet they all distanced themselves from the rest of the Jedi. Most of these little groups consisted of only three of four people, dedicated to the idea of the hermit Jedi. The JU, as it was more commonly known, took steps toward bringing all those of these little rogue groups into one unified Jedi Order, with the JU campus as their main place of interaction. They also took measures to grade the Jedi on a ranking system that seemed fair so that no one could ever just claim a title again. The JU also introduced a physical portion of the testing process, included later in this text; which if you did not complete, you did not pass the test. While the first attempt failed, those of the JU stay ever vigilant, and hopefully, this section will have to be re-written by those that follow me.

The Jediism Movement

J. A. MICHAELS

Showing the Jedi to the World

<u>Jediism</u>: The Jedi religion, focused on acceptance of the Force.

Jediism was a more interesting section of our history. This was the movement to have Jedi accepted as a world religion, or religious faction. In the United Kingdom and Australia, the move was played to have Jedi listed as a religious option on their annual census. While is succeeded in having it put on the census form, it did not mean that Jedi was then an accepted religion. This was a move most Jedi were not happy about, because the general acceptance amongst the Order was that the Jedi was a path, not a religion. The Jedi then were, and still are, based off of an outlook that anyone of any religion can become a student of the Force. The Jedi religion, Jediism, is also a religion within itself, embraced by some Jedi. This does not, however, mean all Jedi must convert to the Jedi religion.   The option is placed before all Jedi, and their choice does not affect their training in any way.

Section Two: Jedi Philosophy
The Beginnings of a Great Jedi

This section will deal with the beliefs and outlook held by the Jedi. From this point on, there will not be any reference to the "sides" of the Force. The student must remember that it is only their intention that governs light or dark. A Jedi is charged with the defense and protection of those around him. To do otherwise is to betray the very essence of being Jedi. This section will begin with the Eight Tenets of the Jedi. These Tenets are what all Jedi must live by in order to be at one with the Force. They are as follows:

The Jedi Code
The Jedi Code is a guideline for behavior at all time. It is put in place to bring the student to an understanding of etiquette amongst the students of the Force. This code is to be followed as strictly as possible at all time. However, as to any rule, there are exceptions to the rule. Be mindful, though...the idea of having exceptions tends to make people find them. Giving in to one's darkness within can cause to a loss of one's purpose, and thus the losing of their path. The most directly understandable way to read this Code for the first time is to start each line with "For a Jedi,..."

> There is no emotion; there is peace.
> There is no doubt; there is resolve.
> There is no ignorance; there is knowledge.
> There is no passion; there is serenity.
> There is no chaos; there is harmony.
> There is no hatred; there is compassion.
> There is no death; there is the Force.

While this tends to be a rather generic and vague code for any one person to follow right away, it is one that encompasses all a Jedi would ever have to face. While there are the exceptions as mentioned above, they are far too extreme to worry about here. I will go into the explanation of each line of the Code instead.

There is no emotion; there is peace.

This line is essential to the Jedi, but it is a misunderstood line. This does NOT mean that one is to act in total stoicism at all time. True, stoic has its time and place, but it is not the ultimate goal of a Jedi. A Jedi is a child of the Force, and the Force is an entity of balance. As such, we should seek balance. Our emotions are natural, and at times, are needed and useful. The point of balance is achieved through understanding of self. When you understand an emotion, and its stimulus, then you will hold control over it, rather than it holding control over you. Then, you can maintain peace in that emotion, and maintain balance.

There is no doubt, there is resolve.

To a Jedi, doubt is a devastating thing. There is a popular phrase from an old fantasy book that states Fear is the mind-killer. This is so terribly true, I felt it only right to include in the proper training of a Jedi. A great Jedi once said "To doubt one's self is only to ensure those doubts." This is an explanation of the vicious cycle that brings about failure in a Jedi. The use of the Force is an act of faith on the part of the student. They do not understand it, and have not experienced it. This, of course, breeds doubts in the student. However, it is these doubts that hold a student back. Doubt and fear are one in the same, because to doubt ones capability to do something is to fear they cannot. Do not let doubts into your mind, or fear into your heart, for they will surely be your undoing.

There is no ignorance; there is knowledge.

This is a line that means many things to a Jedi. First, the surface meaning is that a Jedi should drive for rounded intelligence in all things they have to deal with. They cannot be ignorant of the places they go or the situations they try to help if they can avoid it. This means study hard all aspects of life, not just the Force and the Jedi Way. Learn about anything that one may find useful in some dispute. Learn the law, that is a very important one. A Jedi can do not good if they are in jail. As I said, this line has more than one meaning, and one of its hidden meanings is that through trust in the Force, knowledge is attained. The Force tells us what we need to know when the need arises. It may not come in the form of just instantly knowing, but it might come in the form of stumbling on a book on the ground, or being drawn to read a pamphlet   Even just seeing something can help bring knowledge, helping to 'connect the dots' in your mind. Trust in the Force, and it will teach you much.

There is no passion; there is serenity.

This line reads like the first to the unknowing, but it is far from the same. A passion is an extreme, uncontrollable response to emotional overload. Fear is an emotion, terror is its overload. It is a passion.   Love and Lust lead to obsession and egotism. Sadness leads to despair and depression. The first line teaches to understand these, and thus control them, but they do not pass through an emotional state, they just start a passion. Such as seeing an atrocity, and it causing rage. This is a passion to do harm. Through our self-knowledge, this can be stopped, and the passion can be tamed, making us serene in our understanding of self. This way, the world around us affects us, but does not control us. Our control is to never become passive when faced with a passion of any kind, or we open our hearts to the darkness within ourselves.

There is no chaos; there is harmony.

This is a line that is very important, yet significantly ignored part of the Jedi Code. We, as Jedi, as keepers of the peace. We are not meant to bring discourse, disorder, or chaos to the lives of others. Chaos, confusion, and disorder breed fear, anger, and passion. Chaos is the key that opens the door to a person's inner darkness. Harmony is the maintenance of order, peace, and balance. Harmony in the world is the key to happiness, and a sense of security. Harmony, however, must also be maintained within. Harmony of self, and harmony with the Force.

There is no hatred; there is compassion.

This line does not mean the Jedi have to be "hippies" or "tree-huggers". This does not even mean we cannot kill insects or eat meat. This means we must never hate anyone or anything. Hatred is a dangerous state of mind that removes logic, and gives way to anger, that quickly turns to rage unchecked. We must show a type of reverent compassion to all life, even if it is not meant to stay alive. At times, the Force asks us to end a life, such as a dangerous insect. Now, to kill this one may save several more, but that does not mean you hate that which you kill. Be compassionate for it, and bring its end swiftly. This only does to make the life one with the Force, and make it better for the transition.

FROM NERD TO KNIGHT

There is no death; there is the Force.

This line can be misleading to some. This does not mean being a Jedi will make you live forever. Sorry, folks, hate to break it to you like that. No, this shows that through the Force, our essence will never die. Our soul, our energy, it is part of the Force. As such, we are luminous beings encased in a shell tissue and organs, skin and bones. When the body dies, we do not die, but rather we move on to a higher plane of existence. We become one with the Force. Through this, we live on in all Jedi...in all life. What better fate could a child of the Force have, but to live on for all time as part of all its children. The same is true of you. You are made up of an infinite number of the Force's children, their energies recycled back into the Force itself, maintaining its strength.

One must be at peace to touch the Force,
and must not doubt it in themselves,
and will learn from it,
but must not use the knowledge passionately,
or to cause chaos with that knowledge,
and must show compassion to all life,
for all life is the Force.

The Eight Tenets of the Jedi

A Jedi:
Respects and protects ALL life in its many forms,
Knows the importance of knowledge and seeks understanding on all levels,
Trains to the best of their abilities to use the Force for the greater good,

Commands their emotions and maintains inner peace,
Works to enlighten others when possible,
Maintains high morals and ethics and acts accordingly,
Is open minded and mindful of those around them,
Is free to express themselves as they serve the Force.

These are ideals which I feel should be held by all Jedi no matter what path they are on. I wrote them so that we can all have something to help guide us through our daily lives as we live the life of a Jedi in the real world. They can help us to make decisions and serve as a reminder of how we, the Jedi, should act and treat others. These ideals are not laws or rules, but only guidelines, which we can relate to in the real world, which we work in as Jedi. I hope they will inspire you all to move to greater heights.

Respects and protects ALL life in its many forms.
A Jedi understands that each life in the world is important, has its place and reason for being. The Force is an expression of life and unifies all life together, we are one with each other and therefore harm to another life is doing harm to ourselves. As Jedi we should strive to protect life, as each is a sacred object, which helps to expand and express the Force, therefore it should be treated as such. This also includes plants, animals and insects.

Knows the importance of knowledge and seeks understanding on all levels.
One of a Jedi's greatest possessions is knowledge. It allows us to grow and become a better person, which in turn allows us to be better Jedi. How many great leaders in our world have not been wise beyond their years? Knowledge allows us to help, lead, teach and protect those around us, all of which are part of a Jedi's duty, therefore seek out knowledge of all topics from many different sources. You should never stop learning, as there is always more

out there and relearning something often yields a deeper understanding. Understanding can be seen as an extension of knowledge, taking it to the next level. You can have knowledge of the parts of a car, but do you understand how it all works? Understanding can be applied to concepts, which are not as tangible as others. For example, there are no guidelines about how people interact and what causes people to act in certain ways. But by understanding a person, you are able to see why they act the way they do, this understanding can not be gained from text books which tend to generalize things like this.

Trains to the best of their abilities to use the Force for the greater good.

A Jedi should always strive to learn as much as they can about the Force. A Jedi strives to protect people and with the Force they are better able to do so. The greater the Jedi's abilities in the Force, the better they can help and protect those around them. A Jedi should always use the Force for the greater good, which means that a Jedi may use the Force in any means necessary as long as it is for the good of the masses. A Jedi should always seek the most peaceful of solutions at all times and resort to aggressive means as a FINAL RESORT.

Commands their emotions and maintains inner peace.

There is a wide range of emotions out there and all abilities in the Force are dependent on some sort of emotion. It is okay for a Jedi to express whatever emotion they are feeling, but a Jedi must ALWAYS command and control their emotions rather then the emotions controlling them. Use each emotion properly and in the appropriate situation, but remember there is always more then one way to achieve a goal. You should only use anger when it is TOTALLY necessary and not because it gets you what you want quickly. A Jedi should find the most peaceful path to prevent disturbing the balance of the Force. This means that a Jedi should remain calm and peaceful at all times, and use other emotions only when it is absolutely necessary to achieve a goal.

Works to enlighten others when possible.
We are Jedi because we have achieved a level of knowledge and growth in our life; because of this our lives are blessed by the Force. This knowledge is not something that we should hoard or keep for ourselves; it is universal knowledge, which is there for anyone who dares to seek it out. If someone asks about the Force or anything to do with the Jedi way, that knowledge should be freely given, even if it isn't given through formal training. This knowledge should be given 'when possible' as it is not our place to force our beliefs onto others and tell them that it is THE truth. Help and teach those who are ready for it, allow those who aren't the room and time to grow.

Maintains high morals and ethics.
At all times a Jedi should work to maintain a high level of morals and ethics. We are people who help people and protect the world around them and therefore are respected and looked up to by people. It is only fitting that we act as appropriate role models.

Is open minded and mindful of those around them.
A Jedi should always be open-minded as they go about their lives. We live in a world of infinite possibilities and must be open to the different paths and avenues that we could take in our duties. There are many paths to the top of the mountain and the Jedi must choose the best one, this can be applied to all decisions in life. We must also be mindful of those around us as not to neglect or harm them through our actions or in-actions. Even though we may not mean to, we may physically hurt

someone, insult them, hurt their feelings or disgrace their beliefs without even knowing.

Is free to express themselves as they serve the Force.

A Jedi lives to serve the Force and this is what they should be doing every day of their life, how a Jedi expresses their path is up to them. In this world we all have free will, we are free to make whatever choices we want. We do not have to follow a set of rules or guidelines, therefore a Jedi is free to wear, eat, work, believe and act as they want. No one can force a set of rules or opinions onto you; you are free to express your true self in any way you want. We are all individuals and should express our individualism as we walk the path of the Jedi, making the path individual to each Jedi. This also means that a Jedi is free to forget about these ideals, but with any choice you must also deal with the consequences. Straying from what you feel that Jedi way to be betrays yourself and changes who you are.

JEDI ETHICS

Ethics of Defense

A Jedi is not just a philosophical being meant to theorize about the right and wrong ways to do things such as harming one in the defense of others. They actually have to act on such instances, so that when the situation does arise, they do not spend millennia in contemplation on how to handle it correctly. The Jedi Ethics of Defense were devised for just such a thing. Self-defense according to the Jedi must always comply with certain ethical imperatives. These are many and complex, but for our purposes we have devised situations. In these situations, each situation represents an ethical level of combat. The level rises as we proceed from situation A to situation D. Each situation consists of two men. The man on the left is the Jedi. The man on the right is any other person one might come across.

- In situation A, the Jedi on the left, without provocation and on his own initiative, attacks the other man and kills him. Ethically, this is the lowest of the four levels–unprovoked aggression in the form of a direct attack. Being that a Jedi never attacks first, this particular example is something one should never have to deal with.

- In situation B, the Jedi does not directly attack the other man, but provokes the other man to attack him. It may have been an obvious provocation, such as an insulting remark or the more subtle provocation of a contemptuous attitude. In either case, when the other man is invited to attack and does so, he is killed. While the Jedi is not guilty of launching the actual attack, he is responsible for inciting the other man to attack. There is only a shade of difference ethically between situation A and situation B.

- In situation C, the Jedi neither attacks nor provokes the other man to attack. But, when attacked he defends himself in a subjective manner, i.e., he takes care of only "number one," and the other man is killed or at least seriously injured. Ethically this is a more defensible action than the other two. The Jedi was in no way responsible for the attack, neither directly nor indirectly. His manner of defense, however, while protecting himself from possible harm, resulted in the destruction of another life form. As you can see the result in all three situations– A, B, and C– is identical: A MAN IS

KILLED. Being a Jedi is to be a tool of the Force. Life creates the Force, and as such, to defend the Force, one must defend the life that sustains it.

- In situation D, we have the ultimate in ethical self–defense. Neither attacking nor provoking an attack, the Jedi is attacked. Though he defends himself in such a way, with such skill and control that the attacker is not killed. And in this case he is not even seriously injured. Yet the attacker knows that he will get nowhere by attacking except to sooner or later hurt himself. This last and highest level is the goal of all Jedi self–defense arts. It requires skill: the result of intensive practice of the technical means of defense devised by the Jedi. But it requires more than that...It requires an ethical intention. A Jedi must sincerely desire to defend himself without killing others. A Jedi's goal is to protect life. He must be well on the way toward integration of mind, body, force, of physical means and ethical motives.

He will often have practiced various other disciplines. Breathing exercises and mediation are common means employed in the Jedi Order to further this integration. As we see then, at this ethical level, Jedi emerge as disciples of Coordination, where a Jedi develops his own coordination of mind and body while helping his partner or partners to develop theirs as well.

The practice of the Jedi then becomes a harmonious interaction between two or more people, fulfilling all Jedi's intention via translation of the highest ethics into vital and active modes of conduct. Remember, these are only examples. Each person must decide what they feel is right or wrong in the defense of the

Force, it cannot be taught. These examples only show guidelines of what the Jedi strive to be.

With these ethics of defense in place, a Jedi is charged with the defense of those who cannot defend themselves, or should not have to, the innocent and/or the weak. We are servants of the public, and servants of the Force.

Right or Wrong

A Jedi needs not only the ethics of defense, but an ethical sense of what is right or wrong. That is not a system that can be taught, each person must decide what is right and what is wrong, for each situation is seen differently from each person. It is not up to a governing body to decide what is right or wrong for each person, because to do so takes away their freedom. Just as it was once taught that emotions were the key to the "dark side", that took away freedom of choosing what the Jedi felt was right and wrong. A sense of right-and-wrong is needed because as a protector of the innocent from those that mean to harm them, one must hold conviction that when they are forced to harm the person in the wrong in defense of the one that is innocent, that they are right. This example is not an all-the-time occurrence, but merely an example of an extreme. The sense of right-and-wrong ties very close with the ethics of defense.

Using the Force

Not only does a Jedi need these ethics, but there is also a set of ethics put in place for using the Force. Once more, this set of ethics is only an example, and must be adapted to the person. The Force is a great and powerful tool, and a Jedi needs to understand that while it is their tool, they are also its tool. The will of the Force is carried out by all Jedi, no matter their ethical choices. The power of the Force is a great one, and while it can bring much good to the Jedi, and those around them, it is also as an addictive drug. Dependence on the Force is no better a thing than dependence on someone to do your work for you, because that is what the Force does. The skills taught to a Jedi help them to accomplish things they would otherwise not be able to do. These things include types of meditations, bringing clarity during uncertain times; techniques that allow them to be alert and awake, no matter how little sleep they have actually gotten; and much more demanding techniques, such as that which speeds up reaction time, and allows one to move faster than one could possibly do without the actively-helping hand of the Force. All these skills will be documented later in this text, but for now such examples will be sufficient.

For a Jedi to constantly be in a state off meditative calm makes their choices and actions always calm and well-planned. However, with no experience how to handle things that aren't nearly as dire as a life-or-death situation, when the time comes to do so without the Force, the Jedi will be no better than a wild, panicky animal. Using the Force to assimilate new energy due to lack of sleep, while convenient, it dangerous to the health of a Jedi. Some of the more bold Knights have gone on record of staying awake for nearly a week's time, needing no sleep, and no caffeine to be alert, only the Force. In that time, they lost their appetite, as well as their ability to sleep a full eight hours. These same Knights, when returning to a normal state of being, not depending on the Force for everything; contracted malnutrition because of their dependence on the Force. This was not a good experience for some, but an important one for both them, and you. A Jedi can also use the Force to bypass the limits of their own muscle and physical skill. Such things as increased speed and enhanced strength are only a few of the more advanced skills of a Jedi. Using these skills when they are not totally necessary trains a Jedi to not keep up their physical condition. To do that is to betray the Force by taking its home, and letting it fall apart. These skills can be done two different ways, and both are damaging. One way is to bypass one's muscles, allowing them to wither into a state of atrophy. The other is to use the Force to max out one's muscles, destroying them in such ways as bad strains, pulls, and even torn muscles and ligaments. Excessive use of Force-enhanced running also takes its toll on one's ankles and knees. Anyone who has ever damaged their ankle or knee can tell you, they never fully heal, and the pain never fades. Trusting the Force is a good thing, but turning it into a crutch is not what it means to be a Jedi.

Sanctity of Life

Life, as will be explained in the next section, is the source for a Jedi's power. All life is precious, no matter how small or physically displeasing it may seem. This is why most monks of all religions refuse to as much as step on an ant if they can help it. All life deserves to live, so just because it is within our power to take life, it is not ours to do so with. This, however, conflicts with the Ethics of Defense, where a choice must be made at one point to kill in order to save others. While the lives of the many outweigh the life of the one, it does not make the one life insignificant. Even if killing just one person would save the life of every other person on the planet, it would still be a difficult task for any one man to undertake. One must learn to balance their focus and devotion to allow the scales to decide others fate, while still maintaining their sense of sanctity of life. It is a conflict in being a Jedi, and it is something all must deal with on their own time and in their own way. The samurai used to harden their trainees by having them execute condemned men. The trainees learned to kill at a young age, being forced to cut the heads from living people in order to learn to correctly do so when need be. This training, while seeming quite a bit on the extreme side, was actually a very good tool. This made them face the fact of death, and that they were training to kill someone, very early on. It was smart to have a young samurai trainee kill a man, and freak out about it after the execution...rather than have him freak out after his first kill in the midst of a battle. Killing is not an easy act, and it hardens a persons resolve to sustain life. True, with time, all men become numb to the aspect of killing a fellow man, but that is because they understand when it is needed, and have no problem executing such decisions when the situation comes to bare.

The Force
Energy of Life

What is the Force? Although it sounds like a very simple question, and can be answered with many simple answers, all of those answers would be incomplete, thus making them lies. No matter how truthful one can be, an answer as simple as "an energy field" or "the energy of life", while in their own little way are both true and false. It is an energy field, and this energy is created by life, but the Force is also a feeling, a guide, and a gift to both give and receive. The Force is life and death, good and evil, yin and yang. The Force is all.

Eastern religions have always termed the energy of life as qi/chi/ki. For all intents and purposes, I will only refer to it as qi, yet they are all the same thing. Qi-Gong, energy work, has been practiced by those in the Asian countries for centuries, and their ways are spreading throughout the world like wildfire. These skills include such things as healing techniques, strength/speed enhancement, and improved fighting skills. Some religions have actually devoted themselves to using qi to obtain super-normal fighting skills. While this it a great history of where the act of training the Force came from, it still does not answer the question off where the Force came from or even what it is.

The Force is a divine gift from a higher power. Each religion sees this in their own way. Christians see it as the power of prayer, and the effect it can hold over God's will. Many Eastern religions, such as Taoism, see it as a gift given to those by all living things, as well as what created life. They use it to attain enlightenment, and to purge themselves of all human desires and sins, in hopes that they may go on to a better plane of existence when their body dies. If not, they are reborn to this world, and try again. Although most Jedi do not hold their path as a religion, in a way it is. It holds many of the same religious truths as the other main religions. Life is the creation of some divine power, be it a being, or just an energy. Who is to say what the difference is? It also holds that this energy can be harnessed in a multitude of ways. Conscious manipulation through qi gong, or subconscious manipulation through meditation or prayer, it is all the same. The Force has its hold over reality, and those believe its power to be genuine have their own level of interaction with the Force. It is more an act of seduction than control. When one becomes at one with the Force, they have the ability not to control it, but rather to ask it for help, and the Force will offer its power to those that it favors...almost as if a conscious being.

The powers of the Force are vast and mysterious. They include such minute things as relaxation skills, ranging to such immensely powerful and stressing skills as telekinesis and future-sight. Different skills require different levels of interaction with the Force, and most get easier with time. Some of these skills will even become second nature, such as calming techniques and the ability to focus through such things as pain or fear. A master of the Force is not necessarily the most powerful exponent, but rather the most attuned to the ebb and flow of the Force. A true master has no sense in the Force, because he no longer has a sense of self, merely a sense *of* the Force. As such, his Force presence is immense, yet when looking for a particular person in that presence is a futile act, one will only find an empty shell.

Sphere of Influence

The Sphere of Influence is something all Jedi have, and must understand to properly use their skills in the Force. Basically, the Sphere of Influence is your sensory bubble. Anything within this bubble, you can sense. If you have to be within five feet of a person to sense them, then the radius of your bubble is five feet. That is pretty good for an untrained person, but you are a Jedi, and you must work to be better.

As you train your sensory skills, your bubble will grow on its own. Your mind and energy are used to the heightened amount of sensory information, so the sphere naturally grows to encompass all it can, making the Jedi as aware of their surroundings as it can. Just as the bubble naturally grows, it can also be manipulated into various shapes and sizes. This is one of the ways the sensory enhancement technique works, by shaping and directing your sphere to other areas than normal. The sphere can be flattened and pressed out so as to keep track of multiple attackers, or it can shrink down so as to concentrate the sensing within the now-denser bubble.

The only drawback to the use of the Sphere of Influence is that it is a tell-tale sign of *you*. If you hold your sphere to a massive size, then someone looking for you will know the edge off your sphere touches the edge of theirs. If for some reason you are trying to hide from someone else with enhanced senses, then the recommended action is to pull in the sphere as tight as possible. This will mask you in the Force, but it will also kill your heightened external senses.

Section Three: Jedi Mannerisms
The Act of Being a Jedi

A Jedi is a child of propriety, and being a servant of the people, must have the skills to respectively deal with those they are sworn to protect. The manner in which a Jedi should act is ultimately up to them, but some guidelines will be placed in this text, in hopes that they will help any potential Jedi to make their choice to do the right thing, whatever they decide that to be.

Politeness:
Being polite is a key factor in dealing with other people. Normal people, when shown respect, be it due or not, tend to react better to questions or the intervention of one trying to help, such as a Jedi. Always using a polite mannerism is the best way to reach goals without confrontation, but there are times such things cannot be accomplished.

Respect:
Being polite and respecting a person, while being close, are not the same thing. One's space and possessions can be honored without showing respect. Just because the polite approach did not work and has been abandoned, that does not mean one has the right to just destroy a person's property.

Patience:
Patience is a virtue, as it is said. A Jedi must know patience, because not all things are instant, even within the Force. Patience is needed both in a Jedi's training, and in his duties in the everyday world. Many of the people a Jedi will deal with will be a hurried person, trying to get all they can while they can...a creature without patience. The Jedi should be as a cat, watching

its prey creep ever so slowly towards them. A cat does not get impatient and run wildly at their prey, but rather waits until it nearly walks right into their hands, and *pounce.* This patience paid off. The cat got their prey, and they did it with as little energy needed.

Sanctity of Life:

Closely tied to the Jedi Ethics of Defense, a Jedi must value life in all forms, no matter how grotesque or despicable. It has been said a Jedi is a gardener, choosing what "weeds" are to die in order to let their "favorite flowers" live. This outlook is a matter of personal choice. All life creates the Force, but the lives of the many outweigh the lives of the few or one. If killing one man will save four, do you kill the one, or work towards a way all five survive? Ultimately, it is hoped a way could be found for all five live together, but it is the Jedi's decision of whether to attempt such a feat, or to just strike the one opposing person to guarantee the survival of the others.

Humility:

Humility is something many of the Jedi have been sorely lacking over the past, and it has ultimately been their undoing. A Jedi is a creature of the Force, merely a spec of nothingness in comparison to their creator. To feel as if you are better than those around you, even fellow Jedi...that is to betray the very Force itself. A humble man is one that can ask for help when it is needed, and they can also give help when asked. They are not too good to explain things to those who neither understand, nor terribly *need* to understand.

Temperament:

A Jedi's temperament is another important factor in his mannerism. A Jedi is a public servant, and as such, must have at least an non-offensive temperament to him. While the public may occasionally react negatively to a positive attitude, it will always react negatively to a negative attitude. If a Jedi does not have a pleasant, helpful temperament, then what good are they? If they are not going to help, then no one will ask for that help, making them irrelevant.

Duty:

A Jedi should hold an intense sense of honor and duty. Their first honor should be to the Force, then to those who make up the Force, and lastly to themselves. The Force gives all life the ability to be, and as such, then uses that life to sustain itself. Being a child of the Force, it is the duty of the Jedi to act in the best interests of the Force itself. A Jedi, when their mind is quiet, will "hear" the will of the Force, and out of their loyalty to it, should feel obligated to act upon its will. When the Force has taken one to being under the command of another, their duty is to that person or group. If a Jedi joined one off the many forms of the Armed Forces, despite their geographical location, it is their duty to follow orders, unless the Force tells them otherwise. Lastly, a Jedi should feel a duty to themselves. If they are not under the command of another, and the Force has willed them to make the choice of which path to take, they must be true to themselves and what they wish to be. Duty does not mean one should be blindly loyal to anyone. Through the Force, knowledge is acquired, and that knowledge should be used when dealing with anyone, no matter how drawn to them you may be. Remember, the Jedi's first loyalty is to the Force, and its will. The previous was only an example of how a Jedi's sense of duty should ultimately be. True, no one is perfect. We may be Jedi, but we are still human, and we will all make mistakes. Also, a single Jedi's sense of duty might be different than what is listed above. As long as their sense of duty and loyalty feels right to them, then that it all that matters.

Presentation:
A Jedi should be proud of what they are, and as such, should be well-kept, be it of a clean-cut nature, or of a highly natural look. Short hair, long hair, clean shaven, grizzly beard. It does not matter, but ideally, one would want to keep their personal appearance that of one with pride and composure. People respond better to those who appear to be well under control of who they are, and what they see themselves as, be that regal or rebel.

Appearance:
While closely linked to presentation, appearance is more a matter of what is worn over how it is worn. People respond to appearance more than anything else. Whatever the Jedi chooses as his "robes", this will decide how people treat them. If the Jedi takes the dress of a monk, people will act a certain way, and if the Jedi comes in wearing biker leather and chains, they will react another way. Some may want people to see them as a devout holy man, others may want them to see them as a rebel. This will be decided by their dress, by their appearance. Despite the preaching of "never judging a book by its cover", it is still a part of human nature, and as a Jedi, one must be aware of it as such.

Robes:
Lastly, this brings me with the subject of Jedi Robes. Many Jedi feel that robes are not practical, and as such, there is no reason

for them to have a set. Others believe that the robes are a symbol of a person's dedication to the Jedi way of life, and their creation, pouring who and what the Jedi is into their robes, should be a mandatory experience during the training of a Jedi. It would also do to give the Jedi something "formal" to wear to a gathering of Jedi. This is yet another decision a Jedi must face for themselves: formality or function? Whatever the choice, there is no set design for what the robes of a Jedi Knight actually are. They could be a tactical jumpsuit, covered in pockets and hidden areas for various supplies, they could be a martial-arts style tunic, brandishing rich colors and bold patters as the Samurai wore, they could be monk-like robes, designed to show humility and grace...and they could be so much more.

Symbol of the Jedi

The symbol above is what I feel should be adopted as a universal symbol for the Jedi, as it signifies all that a Jedi should strive to be, do, and understand. In it is shown the very nature of the Force itself. The symbol itself was given to me in a vision almost 10 years ago, and I have spent this time devising what exactly this symbol meant to myself and to the Jedi.

It is simple, and humble, showing a humility all Jedi should strive to learn from. It is simple, dignified, and elegant. No other symbol to date has demonstrated such traits. To date, the largest symbols usually include things like stars, yin yangs, or worst of all, lightsabers.

As of late, some symbols have come about that do not fit these characteristics, but they are not as inspired as this. It also seems to resemble a crescent moon, and this was intentional. A crescent moon is a very common symbol of other metaphysical sects, and this shows a universal unity between the Jedi and other traditions.

The stars, usually held in rings or moons, show some form of hidden knowledge. This is in the case of a dedicated Jedi, a very factual symbol. However, to show it seems to be some sort of egotism, and thus removes the "hidden" aspect of hidden knowledge. In not showing this grand form of cosmic understanding, and instead having the center empty, it shows how much we all have to learn.

Yin yangs, while a very recognized symbol of the metaphysical and martial arts, is a symbol that should be abandoned within the Jedi. It perpetuates an outlook of duality that the Jedi has discarded. The yin yang is a very misleading symbol when it comes to the Jedi. They are also too vague to be associated with just the Jedi.

Lightsabers are just not something that should be in the Jedi of Earth anymore. Their existence to this point in the Community thus far has done nothing but harm the appearance of the Jedi. The removal of that symbol does to distance us from our fictional counterparts.

The symbol is also a ring, holding no faces, as Arthur's roundtable. It shows that the Force plays no favorites, and takes no sides, and the Jedi should learn to be the same way...a lifelong struggle, surely.

It shows the wheel of time, having no beginning and no end. It shows the repetition of the ages, all different, yet all the same. It shows that even in our strongest times [thick bottom] or our weakest times [thin top], we are all still connected, both to one another and to the Force. This is done to give us strength.

The black in the center also shows the universe in its entirety, and the silver ring is the Force, chosen gray to show its balance of light and darkness, thus removing the notion of a bipolar entity. It is also larger than the black, easily enveloping all we know as the universe, and still being larger...as the Force proves itself to be day after day.

Section Four: Physical / Martial Training
Maintaining a Jedi Physique

A Jedi is a creature of the Force, and as such, their body is merely a tool of the Force, a glorious weapon used for a higher purpose. Which kind of weapon would you rather use, one with a blade of heavy, soft lead; or one with a blade of razor edged, ultralight titanium? If you said lead, leave. Right now. Close this text, return it to whoever you got it from, and do not read any further. It is the duty of a Jedi to stay in peak physical condition. As mentioned before, those of the Jedi United had devised an extremely strict set of physical requirements for the ranking of a Jedi trainee. Strict in the fact that you *must* meet the requirements, not that the requirements are outrageous.

Physical Requirements:
Initiates:
Running: 1 Mile run in 9 minutes
Pushups: 2 sets of 20
Crunches: 2 sets of 30
Pull-ups: 2
Bent-arm hang: Amount of time you can hold it
Sit and Reach: Shins hold for 10 seconds
Swimming: 100 meters, any stroke
Treading water: 2 minutes
Squats/Knee bends: 2 sets of 15
Leg Lifts: 2 sets of 10
Martial: None

Apprentice:
Running: 2 Mile run in 19 minutes
Pushups: 3 sets of 30

FROM NERD TO KNIGHT

Crunches: 3 sets of 45
Pull-ups: 3
Bent-arm hang: 15 seconds over your previous time
Sit and Reach: Ankles hold for 10 seconds
Swimming: 100 meters twice(any stroke)
Treading water: 3 minutes
Squats/Knee bends: 3 sets of 20
Leg Lifts: 3 sets of 15
Martial: Basic Self-Defense

Jedi:
Running: 3 Miles run in 25 minutes
Pushups: 8 sets of 45
Crunches: 8 sets of 60
Pull-ups: 6
Bent-arm hang: 30 seconds over your previous time
Sit and Reach: Toes hold for 90 seconds
Swimming: Swimming: 100 meter twice(Once any stroke, second time with object in tow)*
Treading water: 6 minutes
Squats/Knee bends: 10 sets of 30
Leg Lifts: 8 sets of 25
One-legged Stance: 2 minutes w/various hand techniques
Martial: Effective defense of self and others: Empty-handed and w/Baton
Object to be determined.

Master Jedi:
** To be determined upon examination **

Beyond just the physical fitness requirements, the Jedi also require the study of creditable martial arts. They don't have to be traditional, just make sure they work in real situations. The best arts found for combat effectiveness are wing chun, krav maga, and stick-fighting such as escrima and kali. Upon founding a Jedi Training Center, a Jedi martial art will be formed, focusing on the use of the Force as a combat weapon, buy also working hand-to-hand and weapon skills without the help of the Force, so that a Jedi does not become dependent on the Force for their entire fighting prowess.

A Jedi Knight should be skilled hand-to-hand combat, acrobatics, and grappling, as well as the use of the following weapons: staff, baton, knife, keychain, sword. All of practical use except for the sword, which will be used more for discipline and commitment than any actual combat. However, the principles of the sword can be used with a fighting cane or meter-long walking stick. Also, a hardwood practice sword, called a *bokuto*, can be carried openly in most areas. Please check with local law before dragging your practice-sword around town with you, though.

Until the Jedi martial art is founded, it is the responsibility of the student, and of their teacher, to make sure at least some combat skills are instilled. Using the Force alone is not a safe option. The Force is powerful, as is it's children. The only problem is that its strength is elusive to most, and so they must know how to defend themselves at the very least.

Section Five: Techniques
Using the Force

This is the section dedicated to the skills of the Force, learned and used by the Jedi. First, however, one must understand how to use the Force. All Jedi skills are broken into three main groups, the latter building upon its former. These groups are Control, Sense, and Alter. **Control** skills are more internal skills, simple as just being able to direct your internal energies to a certain area of your body. These skills also include those used in controlling one's mind in a crisis. The second level of skill, **Sense**, is when one extends their energy outside of themselves to learn about things other than what is inside of them. This sense skills are such things as empathy or telepathy. These skills require the ability to control one's own energy before trying to understand that of others. **Alter** skills are the most difficult for a Jedi to learn, let alone master. Alter skills include such things as thought manipulation and physical telekinesis.

Using the Force sounds easy. While it can be the most natural thing in the world, it can also prove to be the most challenging. All children of the Force have the ability to command its energies, but some are given more natural talent with it than others. It has been this occurrence that has sustained the Jedi to this point. Each person is made differently, and as such, these skills may come easier to some than others. The most important thing to worry about is that doubt and fear are what stop people from reaching great things. A wise man once said, "To doubt one's self is only to ensure those doubts." This man went on to influence the Jedi profoundly, as can be seen within the pages of this text. This wise man also held the philosophy of power being psycho-somatic, which means it is all an illusion of the mind. If one feels they are weak, they will be. If one feels they can do anything, most of the time, they can.

The first skill one must learn is to feel the ebb and flow of the Force itself. To do this may take some time, and it may not. First, on must open themselves to the understanding that the Force does exist. If one doubts the Force's existence, or their ability to interact with it, then they will fail. Remember, to doubt one's self is only to ensure those doubts. Relax, and feel your blood flowing in your veins. Feel your heart beat, and feel your body shift as you breathe. Next, feel below all of that to the constant tingling of your body's natural energy. The feeling has been described as a tickling, tingling sensation that makes your spine shiver while bringing a smile to your lips. Opening yourself fully to the Force for the first time can be the most invigorating experience in a person's life. You feel as if you are floating, and everything you see is a part of you. That sensation is the ultimate truth, because all things, living or inanimate are a part of the Force on some level. All matter in existence is merely various vibrations of energy fields. Everything is energy, everything is the Force. Some such places are out of the spectrum of a human's ability to sense and/or interact within the Force, but the fact still remains that all things are of the Force.

Something else to remember is that there are two places a Jedi can draw the Force from. One is their internal reservoir of the Force. This is a limited amount of Force energy stored in a person's body. The amount, while still limited, grows as a Jedi grows in skill and harmony with the Force. The other is the infinite rivers of the Force. This energy is drawn at various rates. It could be a mere trickle, tickling the back of your mind, or it could be a full tsunami of energy, flowing into you as fast and as hard as your body can withstand.

Control
Skills of the Inner Jedi

Below will be listed some very basic Control skills. This is list is far from all-inclusive, nor was it ever intended to be.

Calming Breath

Once you have experienced the sensation that is the Force, you are ready to put all that power to use. We shall start with the ability to calm yourself. This is a breathing technique that when mastered, cannot be detected to the untrained eye. This breathing technique can also be used to draw in the Force when making a connection is proving to be difficult.

When first learning this skill, you must already be in a comfortable area, in relaxed dress. It is difficult to learn a relaxation technique when one is too tense to concentrate that long. Lie on the floor or on a bed, somewhere you are comfortable and your back is straight.

Breathe in and out with only your lower torso. When you do this, it should appear as if you are forming a beer-belly. That is fine, just keep breathing. Anyone that has taken any type of traditional martial art should know well this type of breathing.

Once comfortable with the belly-breathing, now breathe in and out with just your upper chest area. Puff up like a body-builder trying to show off his chest. Continue this type of breathing until you are comfortable with it.

Now, we unify the two type of breathing. We are now going to move into what is called a four-fold breath. It is where you breathe in for four counts, hold for four counts, breath out for four counts, and hold your lungs empty for four counts. When written, it looks like this 4-4-4-4: 4 in, 4 hold, 4 out, 4 hold. On the 4-count in, the first two counts, breathe in with your lower gut. On counts three and four, still holding air from one and two, breathe in with your upper chest. Hold all air for the next four count. Now, when breathing out, on counts one and two, breathe out from the upper chest, then on three and four, exhale with lower gut. Then, hold empty lungs for another four count.

Once comfortable with the technique, if it doesn't have the desired effect, such as it didn't calm you as much as you needed, repeat the technique, but this time use a 4-7-8-4 pattern: 4 in, 7 hold, 8 out, 4 hold. On the 4-count in, the first two counts, breathe in with your lower gut. On counts three and four, still holding air from one and two, breathe in with your upper chest. Hold all air for the 7-count. On the 8-count for out, the first four counts are chest, counts 5-8 are lower gut. Then, hold empty lungs for another four count.

Pain Suppression

This technique varies in difficulty, ranging from the type of pain, and in some instances, attempting the technique will only bring more pain, such as in the case of a migraine. This technique requires concentration, and when in pain, that can be a rare commodity, but a disciplined Jedi can pull off such a feat.

First step is to locate the source of the pain. True, if it is a cut or a bruise, it will be extremely easy to locate, but if it is a pinched nerve or pulled muscle, the pain can spread far beyond the injury. Do not only find the pain on the physical, one must also locate the pain with the Force. This will take the most concentration, because as the pain intensifies, the ability to continue on becomes harder and harder.

Once the pain has been located through the Force, the next step is to understand the pain. Learn from it, befriend it, become one with the pain. Allow the pain to travel throughout your entire self. Learn from the pain, and savor it. Cherish the pain as a signal that you are still alive.

Finally, unthink the pain. Once you have learned to understand the pain, think it away. I take that back, *will* it away. This is within the powers of the Force, and so it is within the power of a Jedi.

Once one has learned to suppress pain they can begin to work on such things as contortive escape techniques and battle meditation.

Absorb Energy

This skill can be used to do a lot of things, such as absorb and assimilate the energy of heat, or of other Force-users. A Jedi can draw their strength from the Force, but heat is a form of energy already, so using heat to fuel their amount of internal Force energy can be a quick and easy way to regenerate lost internal energy. Some Force-skilled people will attempt to attack body, mind, or connection to the Force without their physical being. This is a good technique for replenishing the internal supply of Force energy one has, and strengthening their bond with the rivers of the Force.

WARNING: Not all Jedi have this ability, so if you cannot do it at all, do not keep attempting it until you hurt yourself very seriously.

This will be a difficult, and potentially dangerous trick to learn, but no pain, no gain. The safest place to try this would be in a shower of hot-tub...possibly a steam room or sauna. We will begin by learning this skill by taking in heat energy, and making it our own. Remember, all things are one, and all things are of the Force.

Open your mind to the fact that heat is just energy, and that all energy is the Force. Second, slowly expose yourself to a substantially higher amount of heat. Keep yourself calm, and breathe. Let the Force flow through you, and do not shun the heat. Allow your body to take in the heat, raising its own body temperature to that of the water/air. If you are comfortable doing so, and have the ability to do so, once you have become at one with the amount of heat energy in the room, make it higher.

Now, the human body does this on its own to an extent, so don't think just because you can do it in the shower or the sauna that this is a skill you have mastered. The next test is fire. Now, if you didn't do well with the first part, STOP DOING THIS!!! The training of a Jedi should not cause more damage than good, so don't keep hurting yourself. For those who feel they are ready to continue, please light a candle, in a room with no breeze, so that the flame might grow rather large. Now, placing you hand in front of the candle's top, draw in as much energy as you can, and watch the candle. Don't breathe through your mouth, because that will move the flame. Breathe down through your nose, and do so very lightly. As you draw in, if the flame moves towards your hand and begins to grow dim, then you are successfully absorbing the heat energy. If you are just burning your hand, then pull away and stick to water.

FYI: Heat is not the only thing that energy can be absorbed from, but despite the media, the technique is the same.

Force of Will

This skill is designed to use only against attacks from other Force-users, which outside of training, will be rare. This skill is pretty much just a battle of mind-versus-mind. In fact, there is no real technique for it. Just remember this, a Jedi's ally is the Force, and that ally is powerful indeed. Will is psychosomatic, meaning that if you believe you will win more than the other person believes they will win, then guess what.....chances are more likely that you will win. I guarantee nothing, but this skill is just a trick of the mind.

Refreshing

The Jedi ability to refresh themselves is a very valued skill. It is what gives a Jedi their immense ability to have seemingly-endless stamina. Just a light touch of the Force can refresh a Jedi almost instantly, like a deep breath of cool, crisp mountain air. The effect is far from ever-lasting, but it serves its purpose well.

This is a simple technique. Simply open yourself to the Force, and let it flow through you. Use its energies to push away weariness and fatigue, leaving you alert and alive. Even after the connection has tapered down again, the energy will still be inside of you.

Enhance Ability

This is a skill used to enhance physical skill or endurance. It is similar to a refreshing technique, but not exactly. First, open a connection to the Force, and gather as much energy as you can.

Once you have a good link to the Force, then begin whatever task you need to enhance. As you strain at the task, feed the Force into the muscles of your body being used, and also use the Force to protect the bones and joints of the surrounding area so as to minimize strain or damage. Do not just feed all the energy into it, because you do not want to overdo the activity. No matter how hard you will it not to, overdoing the task will cause you harm or damage.

If you do not have enough energy to do the task, and it *must* be done, open yourself to the Force fully while performing the act, and allow it to push you above and beyond your physical limitations, but beware of side-effects later. Using too much energy too fast can cause burnout, which damages your ability to use the Force, possibly permanently.

Accelerated Healing

This technique is used to increase the speed a person heals from an injury or infection. It requires merely opening yourself to the Force, and finding the location of the ailment.

If it is an injury, such as a bruise or cut, both using the Force to direct your T4 cells to that area of your body, but also to wash away the pain and negative energy can increase the speed of the healing in one location. If it is many small injuries all located in the same area, just make the area where the Force is assimilating the negative energy large enough to encompass them all.

In the case of an infection, allow the Force to wash away all the negative energy from your entire body, and continue to do that. That will kill off the infection, because infections live off of negative energy, and by removing their food, they starve to death, in a manner of speaking.

Emotional Blocking

This is a technique used to distance yourself from certain emotions. This can be used on any emotion: joy, anger, lust, rage, love, depression, etc. The example will show the technique being used by a man on love.

First, one must realize the stimulus for the emotion. In this case, the love is to be caused by a woman. This woman has taken his very heart, and he would do anything for her. She, however, does not return these feelings. This makes his longing for her even more. He is physically lustful of her, but it goes so far beyond that.

Next, one must separate the relating emotions from one another. This man must separate his love for the woman from his lust for her.

Finally, one must encase the emotion in an unbreakable shell of hardened Force energy. He takes all his love for this woman, and hides it away from even himself. In time, without nourishment, the love dies, and the man is free from his addiction to this forbidden love. While the physical lust is still there, the man replaces his love for the woman with disgust, and lets that stay, shielding him from her sway over his heart.

This technique is an extremely powerful technique, and it is highly difficult to reverse until it has run its course. This can be done to varying degrees for different effects. If a person wishes to feed off their anger, they would separate their anger from the rest of their emotions, but this time they would encase the rest of the emotions for the time being. The span of emotional loss depends on the strength of the encasement, and the depths at which the emotion is stored.

Meditation

In its most basic form, meditation is the quieting of one's mind, and searching for an answer. Many types of meditation could be listed here, but that would take an entire lifetime to list. A meditation can be aimed towards any goal one sees fit. While the end result is different, the technique is basically the same, with only minor changes.

FROM NERD TO KNIGHT

Begin by sitting on the floor, on a cushion, or in a chair. One can even lie down on a bed, couch, or floor if that makes them more comfortable. The important part is that the back be straight, no matter the location. For all intents and purposes, the technique will be explained as if sitting cross-legged on the floor or on a cushion.

Keep your back straight from your pelvis to your neck, bowing your head, and closing your eyes. Place your left hand loosely inside of your right, with your fingers relaxed and your thumbs pressing against one another, and place them both in your lap.

Allow your mind to quiet, and feel the Force flow though every part of your very being. Envision your body as it floats in a sea off gold...the Force. As you breathe, fill the empty jar that is yourself with the Force. This may take a few breaths to accomplish, but keep at it.

Once your body is at one with the Force, just sit. Sit in the silence and refresh your senses in the calm golden sea of Force. Continue on with whatever you began this meditation for. If you did so only to meditate, then keep your mind quiet, and allow the Force to flow through you as if you were not even there. if you search guidance, ask the question, and listen for the answer, for it may take time.

Sense
Understanding the Ways of the Force

Below will be listed some very basic Sense skills. This is list is far from all-inclusive, nor was it ever intended to be.

Jedi Sensing

This is the most basic Sense skill a Jedi possess, and all Jedi possess it. This the ability to sense the going-ons of the world. This lets you locate things and people in the Force, as well as understand the changes of the flow of the Force.

This skill just required letting your senses expand beyond you. If you have truly touched the Force, you have experienced this, feeling that everything around you was part of you. This was you sensing the Force in all things, just as it is in you.

Sphere of Influence

This is more a lesson of understanding than explaining a skill. The Force, like all other forms of energy, is formless. However, a Jedi has a center, because we are made of crude matter. This energy emanates from our center, and does so in a spherical shape. This makes up our sphere of influence. Anything within that sphere, we sense as fully as possible, and as such, it is part of us, making us responsible for it.

This sphere, with concentration, can be drawn in, expanded, and even molded into non-spherical shapes, such as a wedge or a disc. The shape and size just depends on the situation, and is molded by the Jedi.

There is no way to tell one how to mold their sphere, merely to practice until they do. The skill is not needed, but it is definitely a good skill to have.

Danger Sense

This is a skill valued by the Jedi, because it alters you to dangers around you, more directly, dangers *to* you. The Force favors those who follow its will, and as such, keeps them safe. Just keep a connection to the Force, and it will happen on its own.

However, this is a sense that must be trained, not to develop it, but rather to recognize it when it happens. The Japanese ninja develop this skill, but only after much training. In some styles, the sensing of danger is one of the higher level black belt tests. The *sensei* stands over the one testing, and when he swings, the student either senses the attack, rolls, and passes, or they do not sense the attack, and get conked on the head, thus failing their test. Their type of attunement to the Force does not allow for this sense immediately.

Empathy

This skill is used to feel and understand emotions further than with merely body language and intuition. This is a skill that can make negotiations much easier, knowing how a person is feeling and when/if their hostility is beginning to grow or lessen.

Most Jedi possess this skills naturally, and it takes little more than refining. All one must do to refine empathy is to have someone to train with that is good at channeling their emotions, and as they channel an emotion, you try and see what it is. When you get it wrong, learn from it and try again.

Some empathic signals are flat out wrong, because each person experiences emotions differently than the next. If the signal you are getting does not match the body language or temperament, be wary. You may be 100% on the ball about your empathic signals, or you may be flat out off.

Receptive Telepathy

Receptive Telepathy is a skill used when gaining information from a person. It is not as much probing as it is just listening to the person's mind. Stray thoughts wander from those with an open mind, and in this day, most minds are wide open, and just ready for the reading.

All this takes is quieting your mind and reaching out with the Force beyond yourself, and to the other person. Do not invade their mind, just kind of hitch a ride on their thought processes. You may not catch everything, but you can very easily gather all the information you need at that point in time.

Sensing Force Potential

This is a great skill to have in these days of so few Jedi, yet so many open minds. This is a skill some have and some don't, but as far as I've seen, it is a highly common skill. It is merely an expansion on the basic sensing technique.

As you will soon experience, different people *feel* differently to your senses. Some feel shallow, and empty, others will feel as if they are a hundred meters tall, and made of pure light. There will be some that feel like dark clouds of thick shadow, and others will feel like happy little wisps of sunlight. These are merely examples from my own experiences, and as such, I am sure they will feel different to each person. The point is that different sensations mean different things.

Sensing a person with Force potential is likely the easiest thing in the world. All people have the ability to command the Force, but for some it will be easier. If you know for a fact that this person has never trained in the Jedi arts, yet uses minor Jedi skills already, that is a good sign. If they have the sense of a ten meter person crammed into a two meter body, that is also a good sign. Another way to do it is to phase your eyes out so that you can see energy moving around the person. When that happens, if the energy around them flows freely, and once more, you know they have had no training, that is another good sign. Those that feel like a walking storm are usually strong within the Force, but tend to be more dangerous to train than those who have good sensations about them. If you want to train someone that will be immensely powerful, and highly skilled, then go for the walking storm-cloud.

There are many different ways to experience the sensing of Force potential, and for each person, they will all be a little different. When training, if you train with someone, try and sense how there energy moves and feels, then apply that same sense to the untrained world. The important thing to remember is that, no matter the results of this sensing exercise, all people have the ability to become Jedi...some will just have to work a little harder than others.

Sensory Enhancement

The Force is a powerful gift indeed. Not only can it help to increase physical attributes such as strength, but it can also enhance your natural senses. The Force has been known to enhance hearing, sharpen eyesight, and even "program" your nose to pick up certain smells.

This is not a hard skill, but it is not one easily put into words, so training examples will have to do. The ability to use the Force to enhance senses is merely just a matter of will. When you will your senses to sharpen, they do so. Try concentrating on a spot on the wall. Focus on it, feed the Force into your eyes, and look. After a short time, the point may grow in size, detail, or both.

Next light three candles. Two strong scents, and one light scent. Smell each one before lighting it, smelling the light scented candle last, so its scent stays on your mind. After lighting them, make a conscious effort to pick out just that one light scent amongst the two stronger ones.

Third, let us work on hearing. Have three people stand on the other side of the room, and whisper the same three lines in order to one another. Do not look at them, close your eyes even. Pour the Force out of your ear and towards them in a thick fog. Once there, pull their words back to your mind on a frenzied current in this fog.

FROM NERD TO KNIGHT

Four, work on taste. Any chef already does this on their own, but we are Jedi, and not all Jedi are seasoned chefs. Have a partner make three dishes, all identical. After which, they add one extra spice to two of them. Say one is garlic, other is oregano, and the third is the control group. Be sure to know which is the control, so that you have a way to taste it without interference. Work on recognizing what should not be in the dish, rather that what is there.

Lastly, touch. This one is trickier to train, because more people have very dully sensitive fingertips. In this age of typing, the fingers are worn down with the constant pounding of key after key, and the nerves are damaged due to carpel tunnel damage. However, this will not stop us, for we are Jedi, and the children of the Force. Go to the bank, give the teller fifty dollars, and have her return it in one $20, two $10, three $5, and five $1; making sure there is at lease one crisp bill in each denomination. Once home, someone lay the bills out on a table in random order, and you feel the corners. The ink on a dollar bill is thick enough to feel, but only through intense concentration, or through the hands of the Force, can one read the bill with their hands. Blind people do so because they have redirected the energy from their eyes to the fingertips and hands, making them more sensitive.

All the examples I have listed sound easy enough, but they are far from actions of mere whims. This will must be trained, or the results of these attempts will not be up to par when they really matter. Remember that doubts hold you back, so do not think you cannot do something, because then you truly cannot.

Farsight

The skill of Farsight is a very complex skill, it covers such things as remote viewing, hindsight, and future sight. This can be a trained skill, but it is also a reflex amongst the Jedi. This is more of a meditative state than anything else, and will be taught as such. The skill can be used while not in meditation, but that level of control has be learned through practice.

Drop into a meditation as stated above. Now, decide what you want to do, exactly. If you see the past in a certain place, will it. If you wish to see the future for a certain person, ask for it. If you wish to see a person at that time, reach out to their mind, and listen to it. If you wish to know if someone around you is in danger, extend your danger sense to the entire area. While meditating, power is much easier to both command and receive, and as such, some skills are much easier when done in meditation.

Force Trance

This skill is one that is used to increase the bond of the Force and the Jedi, sometimes permanently. It is not an easy skill, and it may tame some time to get right, so have patience, and all will come in time.

First, one must enter a meditative trance, opening himself fully to the Force. Next, he must align all parts of himself so that they flow in harmony with the Force. Chakra, Meridian, energy centers, one's Center, their mind, their heart, their emotions, *every* aspect of their being. The difficulty is keeping the alignment, because being that you are made of crude matter and a sense of self, your being will resist this alignment....a pity, indeed. The longer you hold perfect alignment with the Force, the more natural it will become.

Once you leave the trance, maintain the balance as much as possible. This will allow the trance to hold much longer. As your mind stays quiet, allow the Force to guide you. Do not fight it, for what it has you do, you must do. Let yourself *be* the Force. Experience the entire universe as if it is part of you, and just let your body be controlled by the Force.

Once you leave the state of alignment, you will not go back to the degree of misalignment you were prior to that. Your self has been used as an outlet of the Force, and has such, has been truly changed by it. Those who have experienced this will feel as if they disappeared within the Force, and sensing them will be nearly impossible.

Alter
Interacting with the World

Below will be listed some very basic Alter skills. This is list is far from all-inclusive, nor was it ever intended to be. The Alter skills will be grouped as one of the following: attack, defense, or neutral.

Force Shield
Defense

This is a skill used in conjunction or in place of energy absorbing, listed above. This is a personal shield that protects every aspect of yourself from an energy attack, such as a mental probe or hostile energy projection/blast. This particular skill should not be projected too far out, because it is more potent the closer it is.

To practice this skill, it is best to find a qi-gong user that is skilled in hostile energy blasts. Once that has been done, place your hands out towards your partner, and push all your Force energy out to the end of your arms. Once it is there, weave it together in a dense, intricate web.

Next, have your partner project their energy at you, and you believe the shield will work. When the attack comes, pay attention to the strong points and weak points of your shield, so that you might train it better.

Once this skill has been developed to a point where one is skilled at it from every angle without extending their arms, attempt to shield someone standing or sitting on the ground next to you. A Jedi's job is to protect others before themselves.

Force Enchanting
Neutral

This is a skill used to create a focusing tool with which a Jedi can do many things. They can make a weapon a part of themselves, making it more natural in their hands. They could also make it where when they hold the weapon, it is much easier to slip into a battle meditation. They could enchant an object to help them calm their raging emotions. This skill could also be used to make a tool for the Jedi to use to increase their output or control of their other Force skills. Below will be listed brief explanations of these four examples. The techniques are nearly identical to one another, but it depends greatly on your state of mind.

When making a weapon a part of you, one must meditate on the weapon, infusing it with your energy in it's most natural state. Pour so much of yourself into the weapon, you no longer sense it as a weapon, but as a living being, living once more through your gift of the Force. This will not make the weapon feel like you, but it will become a part of you, and you a part of it. This will make the weapon understand your intentions better, and as such, it will help you fulfill those intentions.

When using the same weapon to make yourself a battle-tool, the same technique is used, but rather than being in a normal state at the beginning, be rather in a battle meditation. Infuse the weapon with your energy at its most focused, yet most volatile. Fill it with that energy, and when you renew its state of being, it will no longer be merely a part of yourself, but when it is in your hand, it will draw you closer to that state of no-mind that is needed to truly battle.

Transforming something into a tool used for calming emotions is a little trickier, but not too terribly much. Calm the emotions within yourself. Enter a state of emotional void, if possible. Once in that state of pure nothingness, use your energy to awaken the life that lay dormant in your soon-to-be calming object. Then, once it's natural life has returned, instill upon it that same emotional emptiness. Do so until that is all that seems to radiate from the object. *This may need to be done more than once. If you have the object on you, and your emotions are too high for it to calm, the object will fall in sync with your emotional energy.*

Lastly, and my favorite version of this technique, is the creation of a focusing tool. I personally like to use a daily-worn jeweled ring, such as a school ring. Something one can wear everyday without getting bizarre looks. I have also found the opaque gems tend to work better than the clear stones. This time, open yourself totally to the Force, and let it flow through you. Speed up your energy flow and increase your output as much as you can handle. When just on the verge of damage, pour all this potent, volatile energy into your focusing tool. Continue to do this until the energy output of your object matches that of yourself. Slowly bring down your flow, making sure that the object holds its state of absolute flow. This will make it where when you have a very tiny flow, but you focus it through the object, it increases dramatically. Imagine how much higher focusing your full flow through it would be. It would nearly double your Force output.

Force Enhancement
Neutral

This is an expansion on the Enhance Ability skill listed in the Control section. This is, however, a much more powerful expansion. In the precursor technique, one feeds energy into their muscles to increase their skill. In this technique, one uses the Force is a much more direct means. In the case of increasing strength, one would feed energy into the muscles needing strength, as said before. After that, they would use their skills to milk their adrenal gland, pumping their system with liquid strength. Also, they would continue by using their telekinetic skills [if present] to force the object to their will. Focusing through the object and stealing its internal energy tends to momentarily lighten an object as well. A good scream always helps, too.

In the case of speed enhancement, the Force is fed into the neuro-pathways on the brain and spinal column, as well as every fiber of the muscles that need the extra speed. Use the increased energy in the neuro-connections to speed the signals in both directions. Squeeze the adrenal gland so as to increase the "octane" of your blood, using it to also help increase the physical output. Do not be startled at the increase of speed, because doubt will rob you of your connection to the Force, as well as the skill.

Transfer Force
Neutral

This is a skill used when dealing with other Jedi. For instance, if one of the Jedi you are with has skill in some obscure power like Telekinesis or Alter Mind, and despite their total link to the Force, they are having trouble sustaining their effort, this skill takes your energy and gives it to them.

First, have another Jedi with you, and have them use their entire internal reservoir. Next, open your link to the Force as fully as you can. Feel the Force flowing through you as quickly as possible, then take that flow, and rather than storing it within yourself, redirect it to your partner. Allow your link to be his own. This is merely a trick of will.

Drain Force
Attack

This skill is similar to the Force transfer technique above, but it is more aggressive. The Force is a powerful weapon, and as such can do many devastating things. Caution must be taken in using this or any attacking Force skill, because they have the potential to damage very greatly or even kill.

This technique requires merely reaching out with your internal energy to the Force presence of your opponent. Latch onto their Force presence, and slowly begin to draw it away from them. Do not stop there, no. Take this energy, and make it your own. This will leave your opponent weakened, no matter what they try to do.

If they have a shield up, drain the shield using the same basic principles, and use that energy to stun them now that their shield is gone.

Force Harmony
Neutral

This is a skill used when two or more Jedi are trying to accomplish a goal. Not like the Transfer Force, where only one of the Jedi have the skill needed, but a combination of skill. This is used when more than one of the Jedi has a skill needed to complete the task. While others may be transferring their energy, those who have the skill must combine their skills for maximum effect.

First, one must begin to use the skill. For example, I will use projected healing, a skill not covered in this section. After these multiple Jedi begin to use this skill, they must also begin to make their energy flow the same way. The closer the pair, the easier this is.

The energies must combine to become one, thus strengthening the effect. Not only does this help to increase the healing example, but it also keeps "too many hands out of the pot". When doing things like healing, too many personal energies can do more harm than good. When doing other skills, like telekinesis, you don't want two different people pulling from two different spots, pulling against one another and negating the purpose.

《》《》《》《》《》

FROM PATH TO WAY

The fall of JEDI shook the Community hard, and I found myself in the most unlikely of places. It was a site run by a man named Xhaiden. This site was a resurrection of an older site called Jediism, a movement to hold the Jedi Way as a religion. This is an outlook I did not, and do not, totally share. The Jedi Way is a great many things, but it is not a religion. The Force is the religious component. The fictional Jedi came from a monastic order who worshiped and studied the Force. From them, the Jedi Knights were born. Just as knights of the Catholic Church, Knighthood wasn't the religion, Catholicism was. Anyway, Xhaiden was a great many, highly devoted to the Jedi Way, and actually looked on the Path with a religious sense of faith. He even did a radio interview about his site, The Jediism Way.

I was still teaching at SotF at the time, still feeding my students a nugget of understanding at a time. Many dropped out due to impatience. When I wanted them to work on a new skill for a month, I would give them nothing else for an entire month. I lost most of them in month five, just about as JEDI collapsed, when I posted a skill I wanted them to work on for two months straight. Nothing new for two months ran off everyone except my most exceptional online student to date, Jinn. That young man knew the Path better than anyone I have ever met. It was as if it was programmed into his DNA. He was a gift to the Community that, until stable in his understanding, I kept hidden away, allowing him time to become what he and I both wanted him to be, a Jedi Knight.

In the mean time, Xhaiden ran TJW as nothing more than a spiritual community. He was a great administrator, a skill taken from his teaching career offline. He did not tolerate the argumentative ways of the Community at Large, and was swift to expel those who did not follow his code of conduct. He was also a gentle soul, with a great sense of humor. I remember a spree he and I went though, changing people's avatar pictures to other humorous images, such as an ape in shaolin robes, or the Buddy Jesus status from *Dogma*. I remember one rugby player there, we changed it to an image of someone catching a rugby ball in the face so hard the shape of the ball was distorted. It was all in good fun, and everyone laughed.

There were many who called TJW home. Xhaiden, and his wife, whom I called Lady X; the *Matukai* fighter Mindas and his wife-to-be Kitsu; the wizard and Cleric of Thor Lightningstrike, whom we all called Chuckles; a US Army chaplain called Volund Starfire, our rugby player Nick; a young man called Kemaj; the ever-present intentionally-grating Neo; the *Saarai-kaar* of the Jensaarai, Nathan'el; and a rough assortment of others whose names escape me. For those reading this, if I missed you, I am sorry. We all got along well, and while not all of us agreed on everything, we were all civil and we were all friends to one degree or another.

At TJW, I started off with a bang, fresh with insult, but more so with worry, I began to break down the bane of the Jedi Realists Movement. To this day, I thank the first of them for saving this path I love so much from degrading into nothing. However, by that point, I think without the counter-balance of Jediism, the Realists would have destroyed the Jedi with their constant in-fighting and lack of faith. I was acting not out of spite, but as a zealot of the Force as a religion. I am still strongly against the removal of the Force, of the martial arts, and of the Code from the Jedi Way. Without it, what are we besides armchair philosophers and bleeding hearts?

During these years, many things changed in my life and at TJW. For one, I begin to expand my understanding in the Force, through the study of other occult mystery schools. My boss at my security job, Warren, was a great help in this. He is a trained Wiccan, and refers to himself as an Eclectic Christo-Pagan. We had several discussions late into the evening about the similarities and differences between the Jedi Path and other schools of thought, such as Druidry, Wicca, Neo-Paganism, Hermetics, and countless other sects. I even began studying many of these sects, practicing their methods, forging and understanding their tools. I still to this day use my staff in many of my larger energetic self-tests. I find its use as a focus aid supremely helpful. I remember going camping with him one Thanksgiving weekend, and for the first time communing with nature, something I had never done with my studies being solidly digital. I began, after that trip, communing with the various gods and elementals, such as the dragons and the Fae. They are, as all things are, manifestations of the Force. It is all one an the same.

My path of self-expansion bled into the SotF page. I had always intended it to be open to all esoteric sects, but now I was actually accepting the depth of differences between the paths. I placed a section on the site about the use of various focusing tools. I began to use the symbol of the triquetra for the visual representation of the three phases of the Force as I experience them: the Living Force, the Uniting Force, and the Guiding Force. I discussed the use, and misuse, of ritual. I began to incorporate chakra and meridian systems into the teachings, giving physicality to the spiritual. I even took the time to write a follow-up article to an old JotNM article where I denounced magick as "unnatural". I was foolish then, and had become more open in my approach.

So, as the years go by, and Jinn becomes my first and only graduated Jedi Knight. Not just from SotF, but ever online. I have had many direct students, but none have ever made it anywhere near as far as Jinn. He took his calling offline, and began to be a Jedi in his community. I am still to this day proud of his efforts, even though he is no longer staunchly of the Jedi Path. He is, and always will be, a great person for what he has learned. It was with his leaving that I realized, once you begin this path, any religio-philisophical path, you will be forever changed by your experience on that path. You may forsake the active study, but you cannot undo the past.

Students of the Force closed down, and Xhaiden and I had reviewed the successes and downfalls to how I was teaching there, and strove to use the method in a grander scale. We devised the Kharis Institute of the Jedi Way, which we called KI. I dedicated the school to my first teacher, Kharis Nightflyer. We were steadfast, until I had to remove myself from the internet once more due to finances. That left a great load on Xhaiden, and I feel bad for it. KI never officially launched.

TJW eventually dwindled to nothing and Xhaiden closed it for lack of use, and he took a step back for a time. The failure of KI, and the degradation of TJW had taken a toll on his faith, and he had to relook his approach, and find his feet again.

I lost my access to the internet because I moved to an apartment close to my work, because I had no reliable means of transportation. The place was affordable, but just barely. I had to find a roommate, and luckily, I had one. A Jedi student named Gaelin moved to Memphis from Fresno, California in order to train one-on-one with a Jedi he trusted. I am not sure why he picked me, but he did. In truth, he arrived several months ahead of schedule. He had left his family home due to increased tensions between himself and one of his cousins. When he was working, which was about seventy percent of the time he was here, life was very manageable. When he wasn't, things got a little tight. Like, ramen noodles every meal kind of tight. It didn't work out very well, in the long run. He was too stubborn to listen to someone who was, in all truth, younger than him. That, coupled with his sporadic work history, eventually drove a wedge between the two of us. He moved after about eight months to Cleveland, Ohio.

After this, nearly all of my study and development became offline. I continued to study the occult schools of though, as well as many other philosophies. I took a great liking to the eight-fold path of Buddhism, as well as the unique practice of aggressive Dragonic Magick. I have always had a draw to the dragons, so this fit well from the start. I came into contact with my guardian, which due to my focus at the time, expressed itself as a dragon I call Drake. My guardian became intertwined with my metaphysical senses. It was likely always there, but the expression was now more acute. Whenever I would need to look at something, rather than a curious tingly pressure in my eye, it felt like a sharp jab in the side of my neck, and if by a finger. When I would feel danger, rather than the the chill up my spine, I would feel a talon digging slightly into my shoulder, like a pirate captain's parrot. In visions, rather than floating, I would circle as if looking from the eyes of a hawk. I was experiencing my senses from the perspective of my guardian dragon. It added a new look at how the Force worked. I spoke with Warren about my interactions with my guardian, and he said what was going on was normal, to begin to see and feel things through one's guardian. For me, it was a definite first.

I remember a time when, one summer, a particularly nasty storm system pulled through Memphis. At this point, I was still at the apartment across the street from work. This storm began to produce tornadoes, and a lot of them. It was one of the most active storm systems I can remember. I heard there was a funnel cloud headed directly for my job, where I was at the time. I also remember beseeching Draco, father dragon, to protect me and my family. Everywhere the storms were, I had family. I cannot speak for anything more from the sites of my family, but no tornadoes hit. I do know that at work, there was a circle I had cast for protection, and a clear circle of sky above my head. I could see stars. There was no rain, and very little wind at all. The sirens lasted for hours, but once they were gone, I released my request, and the remaining clouds came in. Within less than a minute, a bolt of green lightning, pure static discharge, struck and knocked out all the power at my work and apartment. It was as if by releasing my bubble or protection, the edge decided it was going to slap me just once for stopping the storm. Also, the ring I wore on my hand as a socially-acceptable focusing tool got very hot and blistered part of my finger. I could not remember ever affecting the world around me through the Force to such an extreme. My faith in it, my trust in it, grew ten fold that day.

I also began reading the works of Stuart Wilde, a new age self-help type of writer. His work was straight forward, humorous, and laced with both a light vibe and a lot of heavy material. He dealt with many issues, from causing miracles, to accessing the Force, to the power of silence. He is a great author, and the thing I picked up from him most was the Silent Power of the Warrior Sage.

J. A. MICHAELS

《》《》《》《》《》

LOFTY HEIGHTS

Well, after so many years of various energetic programs and occult schools of practice, I decided to write a book. It wasn't meant to be anything but a test of my knowledge. I outlined a book dealing with the various major forms of energetic work, from reiki, to spellwork, to unaided new age energetics, and everything in between. I filled it with popular images that I found helpful or appealing, such as the triquetra, the Eye of Providence, both the Celtic and Qabalistic Trees of Life, and various other things. I discussed in no particular order: meditation, focus, forging occult tools, raising energetic vibration, communion with guardians and the Higher Self, basic principals of numerology, and several other things. It was roughly a hundred pages, double spaced, and held just a slight glancing over of all the things mentioned. Looking back at it, I am surprised to find nothing of the Jedi in those pages. I think it was due to the fact I was sponging up everything I could get my hands on. My metaphysics book collection quickly started to rival my martial arts book collection, and I think I only wrote about what I had on my shelves, rather than in my mind.

Well, I remember laying out the book, and getting all the images together, and everything. Then, I started to write, and I realized just how little I knew about all of it. The Qabalistic Tree of Life is a good example of this, but not the only one. I was stepping into something that others spent their entire lives contemplating and understanding. I was like a lost child in the Mall of America. I had no idea what I was getting into. I researched everything so much that it all started to blend together in my mind. I was never very happy with the finished product, it was all too short and too shallow. The point I make with this is that I began to see, through unintentional saturation, the true unity in all of it. It made me understand that no matter how one does what they do, it is the intent behind the action that decides what kind of person they are. This realization echoed several things I knew already, about how there was no dark "side" of the Force, just dark intentions, and how the Force is the same, no matter what facet you happen to study.

I think that was the turning point in my studies, and the straightening of my Path. I was Jedi, I am Jedi. I had studied sect after sect of energetics and magick, for years, always with the intention to be a better Jedi, and I just got lost under all the books. I could not see the forest for the trees, so to speak. So, I still use my staff, and I still meditate with my mala. I still wear the Om symbol on my flesh, and I still wear a pentacle from time to time. It mattered not, because I was Jedi. I was set straight, and nothing could ever pull me from my Path. I had returned to my roots, and reclaimed myself. However, I ran into one little speed bump. My heart.

I had, once upon a time, fallen in love. I know, there has been no real mention of positive relationships up to this point, and as much of a bittersweet memory as this is, I came to many interesting discoveries during this time, so I am inclined to include it. By this time, I was diagnosed with my bipolar disorder, with a particular taste for depression. I refused to be medicated ever again, after my ADD medication as a child. So, a little more aware of the situation, I was dealing with it well enough. I had come by a female student, whom I called Joy for more than one reason, and had allowed the student-teacher relationship to develop further than it should have. I know, bad Jedi, but it happened.

At first, it was just an attraction, then a desire to hear her voice. I knew it was not the teacherly thing to do, so I tried to fight it. I tried to keep conversations short, and on topic. One day, that all changed. Joy had scraped together enough courage to say "I love you" over the phone. No one outside of my family had ever said that to me. I did not know how to react, so I just pretended not to hear her, made some excuse like I had dropped the phone or something, and got back on topic. I know, it sounds so callous, but I was dumbfounded. I did not know what to do, I had never had a real lasting relationship, and my training in the Jedi Way, and the dozen or so other paths along the way, had taken up so much time, I had almost forgot to miss human interaction of the intimate nature. I was a serial dater, sometimes making it to a fourth date before some little thing about me ran the women off. The Force, and all it mysteries that I had experienced thus far, did not prepare me for this. Here was a person who knew *me*, inside and out, telling me she loved me.

It took her weeks to bring it up again. She had mentioned trying to tell me before, but repeated my lame excuse as to why I "didn't hear her". I admitted, then, that I had heard her, but I did not know what to say, so I had lied. I remember sitting on the phone, debating with both Joy and myself, about why she thought she loved me. My heart was blind. Even with the short moment I had with my former-instructors daughter, the one I mentioned previously, I had no idea she was starting to become fond of me. She had to tell me, too. She didn't love me, just like me, and I saw how hard it was for her to say something, so still cannot imagine how much courage it took for Joy to say it the first time, more or less the second. That was a level of vulnerability my Dad had beat out of me long before. I don't think I believed in love at that point. I remember telling Joy I had no way to know what I felt about her, and left it at that. I vividly remember how crushed she sounded in that I did not return her love. The truth was, I could have, and was too scared to do it then.

I loved everything about her. I knew it, but I didn't want to tell her because I was afraid of the change it would bring. I didn't want her to change who she was suddenly because we loved each other. I didn't want her to argue points with me less, or submit to a way of thinking simply because that is what I believed. I didn't want to see myself defend my position less because all the sudden, I love her. I did eventually allow myself the vulnerability of telling her. I was scared, and confused by it all. Things did change, but not in any of the ways I feared. No, they got a great deal weirder.

After a few months, I remember one day, I suddenly had a massive craving for dark chocolate. Now, I'm not a huge fan of chocolate. I don't dislike it, but I don't go out of my way to get any. I couldn't figure out why I wanted this chocolate so badly, but I *had* to have some. When I got home from work, Joy called me, and she sounded like she was sick. I didn't think much of it, because I knew this was the week of her cycle. I knew why she didn't feel good, as best any man can. She offhandedly said she hated when she had her cycle, because it made her want to break her diet so badly. When I asked what she meant, she said her one craving during this time was always dark chocolate. A little taken aback, I let the coincidence go for the time being. It happened again, every four weeks. I wanted chocolate, and Joy was entering her cycle. Our energies, even over a distance, had synced up enough that I was feeling, sharing, her craving for chocolate.

It didn't stop there. I remember one night at work, I nearly broke my foot doing something security-related, that my boss has said I cannot disclose. I was in a great deal of pain, and had a serious bit of trouble walking for several days after that. Within minutes of the actual incident, she had called me and asked if I was okay. She had felt her foot start to hurt suddenly, and while she hadn't as much as moved, I had told her about the cravings, and she figured I had done something. We were sharing not just thoughts, but physical sensations. She would wake up at five o'clock in the morning and go for a run, and like clockwork, five in the morning, my eyes would shoot open. I would usually go right back to sleep, but it was there nonetheless. If I didn't wake up, I would ask if she had skipped her run for the day, and sure enough, she had.

Two nights stick out in my mind the most, though. I was lying in bed, talking to her, happier than I had ever been in my entire life. I felt like was floating, and on fire all at once. I was laughing sporadically for no reason whatsoever. All the lights were out, and my blinds were closed, plunging my room into total darkness, like when I meditated. I remember being able to see detail in my room, far more than usual. I looked at my hand, and it was emitting a faint blue light. I was glowing, with happiness of all things. Now, in hindsight, I might have been glowing, or I may have just been at such a heightened state that my senses were insanely clear, I cannot be sure. All I know was I was seventy-five levels passed giddy, and I was glowing a faint blue. I leave it up to you which you believe. I personally don't know.

The other night wasn't as grand in the same way, but was far more powerful a night. I remember Joy had been betrayed by a friend, and she was furious about it. She wanted to exact revenge, and was afraid of the thoughts going through her head. I wasn't often her teacher anymore, but that night, I resumed the role. She said she was worried she would succumb to her negative intentions, and I told her that if she were to ever fall, I would catch her. That was when it happened. One second I was talking to the love of my life, and the next I was in an empty space. Then, I was in the center of an endless tube showing what looked to be television shows. Some moved quickly, others more slowly. Some looked familiar, while others looked very strange. Within an instant, I knew they weren't stations on the TV. They were possible futures. My possible futures. I remember, stepped out of time, watching them all for what felt like forever. It took me a long time to process what all I had seen, but I remember seeing myself killing a man, killing myself, dying by the hand of another while in combat, locked away in prison, meditating in a cave wearing all white, wrapped up in a straight jacket with a wild look in my eyes, and countless others it would take far too long to even briefly describe. The one I remember most was what I took to be my most likely path. The future me was nothing like the me while I was watching him. He was hard, an edge to him that I never quite reached. Beard and mustache, with shaved head screamed in bright contrast to my then-lengthy mane and clean-shaven appearance. He was standing with several other people. I knew they weren't all Jedi, but several were, and all were Knights of some fashion or another. He wore all black, and carried a pistol on one hip, and a large knife, maybe even a short sword, on his back, handle extending down for a weak-side underhand draw. He and his fellow Knights were together, standing in a loose circle, lamenting the death of one of their own, whatever they were. I do not remember a conflict of any kind, but I cannot say for sure there was none.

Then, suddenly, I snapped back to hearing myself say I would catch Joy, and after a moment, I began to cry. She asked what had happened, but I could not tell her. I remembered very little of any of it at that point, it was all a weird mash of images. I just knew I was crying because, of all the possible futures I saw, she wasn't in any of them. I had broken the veil of time, and rather than elation and awe, all it brought me was pain. As I began to recall them all, I would try to insert her into my visions, looking for her, feeling for our connection, and never found anything but an empty hole. Making sense of them all was maddening, and the only ray of hope in my life was nowhere to be found.

I am not going to go into the mess of our eventual break-up, or any details beyond this. They serve this text no purpose. It was not pretty, and it hurt a great deal. Just one more in a lifetime of betrayals. I now see that it is as it had to be, or I would have never gotten here, or anywhere else for that matter. Joy was not meant to be part of my path for the long run. I just hope she is happy where she is now, as we lost touch shortly after I broke our connection. It just hurt too much.

I pulled myself away from people, away from the Force, as I tended to my new set of emotional wounds. I knew then that I would lash out like a wild animal at anyone who tried to console me. I ignored the pain as best I could, at least while at work. I dissected it as best I could when I was home, but in the end, it took time, and a lot of it.

In hindsight, that relationship had taught me an endless number of things. It taught me the highs and lows associated with loving another person selflessly. It showed me beyond any shadow of a doubt the interconnection of all life. It taught me how to let go of things that hurt me, rather than eating them to fuel my pain, as I used to do. It also taught me that the Force doesn't really care what you want, but it will always provide what you need. What one wants and what one needs rarely take each other into account.

《》《》《》《》《》

BACK TO BASICS

To ease my pain, or attempt to vent it at least, I began focusing on my training again. I began sparring with Warren, only using something neither of us had a lot of experience with: *shinai*. To say *shinai* fighting is fun is an understatement. Addictive is likely a better word for it. We decided to follow the role Heib had left, and began to just teach ourselves from the writings of the old masters. It isn't the most effective transmission of understanding, but I think it is a far better way to find true expression. We began working on the three rings of swordplay, as well as the corresponding nine cuts. Simple enough to start, but once you get moving back and forth, and confident in your guard, you start to go harder, and faster, and those split bamboo swords make one hell of a great sound. When two hit one another, it is like thunder. You get a charge to the bone. You strike, and you feel the strike. You miss, and you feel the misses. They sting, more so if on exposed flesh. They are much safer than *bokken*, though, in that *bokken* don't flex. They break things, bones included. And when you are starting out, your fingers get stung a lot. Mine always got caught on the tip of the nail. It is not that I was afraid of the pain. I knew life hurt, so did Warren, but we were both of the mindset that pain for no reason was just really stupid. That is why we were using *shinai*, not *bokken*, or Force forbid, our collapsible steel batons.

I remember getting access to a tennis ball launcher, and deflecting them with my *shinai.* I was trying to allow my senses and reflexes to bat away the bright green rubber balls before my eyes reacted to them. I know, it sounds pretty juvenile, but it was fun, and it was also very doable. Most of the time, I would catch one, miss one, then dodge one without using the bamboo sword. I remember getting five in a row at one point. These sessions of working with swordplay were, and likely still are, some of the best memories I had.

I also dove back to the first page of my training, all the way to my archives of Kharis's Praxeum. I was a boy when I first went there, amazed at the simplicity of the idea. As a young man, looking at them, I was more amazed at the effective simplicity of the actual writings. Kharis was an intelligent man, and a skilled teacher. His words were few, and dripped of an early-movement clinging to the fiction, but they were precise, and they were precisely what was needed. I went back to the beginning again, not because I had lost my path, but this time because I was lost on my path. My pain overshadowed any connection I had. I could not meditate, so I could not focus. With no focus, I could not see the bigger picture, the macrocosm. My pain hand blinded me to everything I knew. If I touched the Force, it amplified my emotional pain into actual physical headaches. I was out of sync, and very much at a loss.

So, I did what I always did when my head was too fuzzy to think. I trained. I trained often, and hard. I bought a water-filled boxing bag, and began working on my striking power again. I even dusted off my gi, and began to do my kata again. No matter how many flashy outfits I make, or have made, I knew then that my gi was my true set of Jedi Robes. I knew that I had progressed further in the Force, and in my path, in that pair of ancient pajamas than all my other robes together, ritual robes included. That was what I needed. That was what all Jedi needed, a discipline to immerse themselves in the Force, to feel the vibrant charge that came from combat. I decided, I cannot remember the exact day, I was going to devise a martial arts system for the Jedi Way. It would exist along side any training I might have done live. It would follow the Code, and the philosophies of the Path. It would exist in shapes, not locked forms, so that the principles were grasped more quickly, and those who learned it would become skilled in its execution far faster than the typical dojo. I realized that I had always seen my combative training as somewhat separate from my Jedi training. It seems ridiculous, but it was true. I had brought it all together, and had come full circle. As a sort of inside joke, I began calling this endeavor *Zenryoku-kai*, the Path of the Full Circle, however the more I worked on it, the more it fit.

After a time, I realized I did not have enough diversity in my combative training to form this full circle, so I have been since then studying as many forms as I can get information on, and training as much as possible in whatever is available This was about the point I decided, several years after I was eligible to do so, to buy my first firearm, and graduate to armed security work, and an armed lifestyle. It wasn't until much later that I realized I was becoming the future me that looked so alien when I first witnessed my vision. So, *Zenryoku-kai* is far from done, it may never be, but I will keep working on it until it is complete, or I am dead.

J. A. MICHAELS

《》《》《》《》《》

THE ONE WHO CAME BEFORE

The title of this chapter is the direct translation of the word *sensei*, a term that loosely equates to "teacher". It is commonly found in the martial arts, as well as the Asian internal healing arts. I pondered this for some time during my stalled development of *Zenryoku-kai*, and began to remember that I came to most of my realizations in the martial arts while teaching others, or reflecting upon something a student asked me I did not know the answer to. So, to further my understanding, I began to teach. Most of it was in my living room, and with friends from work, my boss's kids, and some martial artists I met during my early firearm training.

I experimented with various teaching styles, various systemic goals, and various ranking structures. I never really liked how long the colored ranks were when I was training. As soon as one belt got broken in, I got a new one. I still don't have a good answer on what to do there. Too many ranks, and people focus on their next test, rather than learning. Not enough ranks, or no ranks at all, people did not see their progression, and quit from boredom or a sense of failure. Sometimes, I was a very serious drill instructor type of teacher, others I was detailed in explanation before ever starting the teaching of a technique. I also played the role of the "big brother" type of teacher, rather than a master or *sensei*. I found that different methods works better for different students, and have such began to stay rather neutral for a time while I figure out what teaching personality works best for them.

I held a second degree black belt at that time, when most often a teaching sanction was not offered until third degree, and had neither a direct instructor, or backing organization. So, I went out in search of one, or both. I found a non-style-specific sanctioning body, and applied for membership. When testing for my third-degree promotion, I was shocked to find at the end of the test, which included teaching several students a kata they had never even seen before, that I was awarded fourth degree black belt, because of my time spent as a second degree. I was also given some low-level master honorific that I never use, and really wish I didn't have. I began training again with a dojo locally, and that is where I met my spiritual brother, Tank. I did not stay with this group for long, due to observed harmful training practices. When I left, Tank left with me.

Tank was a second level white belt, what most modern systems would call an orange belt, when we met. He was formerly Air Force Recon, had been a bouncer, an active armed security officer, and a practicing pagan, his emphasis on druidry. His energetics came naturally to him, but since they developed before his understanding of manifestation did, they were a great point of chaos to him. He also had an abusive father who taught him hatred and rage far better than forgiveness and compassion. We were kindred spirits, to say the least.

We began training together often, in the martial arts and in the metaphysical arts. I learned to read and dissect chaotic weaves, taking apart what he made. It was then that I learned there was no such thing as chaos, just patterns too complex to be readily seen. You had to understand the source to read the pattern, and once you could read the pattern, you understood the source of them all the more. I quickly did away with the idea of training him within a rank structure. He already had enough experience with combat, due to past training and job experience, that he did not need work on technique. True, his technique is not technically perfect, but what technique ever truly is? Bruce Lee's techniques were very flawed, but everyone knows how well they worked for him. The things we trained in was tactics, and scenarios. Environments changed, lighting changed, advantages changed. We did not train for more belts, but less bruises. We exchanged ideas on the merits of a straight-forward attack versus those of an angled deflection attack. We worked on the three rings of combat, and the three removals of a conflict. We worked on integrating his energetics into his strikes and blocks, a skill that I gained many bruises from him learning.

The major difference between the two of us is that my life had made me quiet, nearly stoic. He had been raised in the military for the first part of his life, and when his father retired, nothing really changed. This had made him bitter, but he had not developed the go-with-the-flow mentality I had. Instead, he was an alpha male, almost always on the offensive, quick to anger, and ever-ready to defend his position on anything, with physicality if need be. His ego had been damaged as a child, and he found strength in living the life of the solitary wolf. At times, I could feel his rage and pain and sorrow pour out of him so strongly, it made me physically ill. I doubt if he had ever been around another true sensitive, so he would have never known it was happening. I do not say these things to belittle him, but merely to say what he was.

Despite our personality differences, the connection between us was nearly instant, and very strong. For a long time, the sight of one of us meant the presence of the other. We were outcasts of our families, of our social arena, and of ourselves. He will tell you that he does not care, but that is a lie he cannot even make himself believe. He seeks social acceptance, but has always done so in a way I had never seen before. Rather than attempting to conform to social norms, he would intentionally go beyond them, as far as he could. He was not ashamed of who and what he was, no matter how hellish the road there was. He was the epitome of the idea that what will be, will be. He knew, far more than I ever came to realize, that all the speed-bumps on his path were needed to be in the moment he was in. He knew this all instinctively, no one had told him this. He did not read it, and it did not slowly dawn on him. It was just there, right where it was supposed to be.

Tank also showed me something I had been afraid to find out on my own. His charisma, as tainted as it was by his past, was accepted. Sure, people disagreed with him, and sure people questioned some of his actions, but they accepted it as part of him. Even knowing that, they accepted him.

I began to slowly adopt some of this knowledge to myself. I was still Jedi, having not truly left, but I was exploring the depths of my soul since my exile. I was not raging in bipolar down swings, but I would still become depressed. I made it a point to release that depression quickly, even if it meant standing out, raising my voice, or using more profanity in one sentence than I would in a whole week, normally. I began to allow my personality to not be an emotionless drone. I wasn't putting on my social mask in order to leave the house. I wasn't dressing to impress anyone. I began to wear my meditation beads out of the house, and stopped caring what people thought of them. I was taking the steps needed to be happy with myself. I had always noticed a difference between my daily grind and my spiritual self. In life, I was continually a subject. I had taking the meaning of *samurai*, to serve, too literally and had made myself a slave to my surroundings. Inversely, while walking the spiritual path, I was always in a high position of leadership and authority, ever since I struck out from Baal's Academy. I was always teaching, or altering something to make it more complete. I had a prominent voice when it fed through my fingers into a keyboard. I had the mind of an alpha male, but the personality of a beta male. I was a leader who subjugated myself to following others, and quietly feeding their development, so that the one who put forth charisma could do all the actual leading. It worked, but it was not who I was inside. The inner me was expressed only within the Jedi, but a Jedi is not Jedi only when around others like them. They must walk the Path, live the Way, at all times, or they betray all that they know to fear and social pressure.

Then, the greatest part of my growth happened, and as it has been said, growth hurts sometime. This time, I don't know if hurt is the right word.

Three Rings

There are three "rings" formed by your body: Outer, Middle, and Inner. These rings exist as the three ranges of defense, and the three ranges of countering.

OUTER
Hold your leg out in a side kick at hip height. Your foot marks the outer edge of the Outer Ring. In this ring, only kicks and/or highly extended hand strikes can make contact. At this distance, you are in the least danger of the three rings. At the Outer Ring, techniques have a long way to travel, giving you plenty of time to see them and block/deflect/evade them. Know that any counter you offer is at the same hindrance.

MIDDLE
Hold your upper punch out from your shoulder, and you have the fringes of the Outer Ring, and the extreme edge of you Middle Ring. This is the distance where most combat is done. It offers the best offense/defense equilibrium. Blocks are effective, and counters are less obvious. The danger of this ring is moderate, as strikes can connect with serious effect.

INNER
Extend an elbow strike or knee kick, and you have the fringes of the Middle Ring, and the extreme edge of the Inner Ring. Do NOT let someone this close to you in combat! You are in the most danger as defense is almost impossible. The Inner Ring is fast, strong, and highly vulnerable. Many strikes are unseen, and wield devastating potential. This reason is why it IS the best place to be

when on the counter-offensive. It is easy to maintain hold/locks, and even easier to throw from.

Always remember, (baring extreme height differences) if they are in your Outer Ring, you are in their Outer Ring, and so on. Dynamic movement can take you into their closer rings, but the advantage you gain, you give.

The Middle Ring is the best place to be, because you can quickly enter their Inner Ring for a powerful strike, or retreat to the Outer Ring, evading an attack. Be very mindful of spacing.

Three Removals

When forced into a defensive position, there are three steps one should take to maximize efficiency, and make it home that night. These three principles, when trained diligently, will make you martial arts powerful.

–Remove the Gap
–Remove the Centre
–Remove the Threat

GAP
The first thing to remove is the Gap: the distance between your attacker and yourself. This takes courage on your part, built by continuous training. While it sounds dangerous, as all forms of combat essentially are, the strategy of moving in works often in defensive application. Unless a HIGHLY seasoned fighter, most do not operate well in closed quarters. Also, the closer a technique is to your body, the stronger it is.

CENTRE
The next thing to remove is the opponent's Centre: that is their balanced vertical alignment. To have one's Centre, you must have three things in balanced vertical alignment: hips, shoulders, and head. Remove any one of these and the opponent will lose their Centre, this making any further attempts awkward and weak. Be careful, though, not to lose YOUR Centre in the process, or you remove one more thing: your advantage.

THREAT

The third and final thing to remove is the Threat: the ability for an attacker to continue attacking. This can be done on any number of levels, depending on the situation. If someone suffers an emotional loss, they may lash out. In this case, simply thwarting a strike or two can diffuse the situation without ever having to do another any harm. In the case of a bully, a loss of face on his/her part will oftentimes end the confrontation. A true aggressor is a rare thing, but when you find yourself faced with one, they will not stop until one of you is too broken to go on. In this case, do what you must to stop them. You will not make it out untouched. When hit, do not freeze up in pain. This is why training often includes controlled contact, so one can focus passed pain, and continue on until safe.

These words are not meant to scare you, or run you away. They are to prepare you. Yes, a forced defensive position can be a scary thing. Mine is not to paralyze you in fear, but to help you make that fear a tool to be used.

Ko Sho Ittai
All Blocks are Strikes

This string of four characters is my favorite in all the Japanese I have ever been exposed to. They tell the ultimate truth of karate: all blocks are strikes.

This exists on many levels, the first being the design to block hard-to-soft/soft-to-hard. The second is almost as obvious, blocking to atemi points so as to inflict neutralizing pain. Third is that a block is the same as strikes in a universal sense. If you have to block, chances are you failed to do all you could to avoid the confrontation.

There is yet another level, though; one not so easily seen. That is not in speed or power of execution, or in the precision of the maneuver, or in the philosophical abstract of personal failings. It is in your fighting spirit.

One's spirit must be large to strike hard, fast, and accurately. A block requires the same spirit: the same courage. One must never be afraid to block an attack. Yes, it might hurt you, but you had be doing your best to return the favor.

The difference can be seen comparing blocks as one progresses. At white belt, blocks meet at the wrist. At green belt, they meet just behind the wrist. At brown belt, blocks meet well into the forearm. By black belt, blocks meet at or around the elbow.

The further in one blocks, the more they risk if they miss, and the more they gain if they succeed. It takes less effort to divert a punch from the attacker's elbow than from their wrist. It takes courage, honed by diligent training, to be able to truly move into a block.

Something to think on when next you here "Ko Sho Ittai".

Living in the Higher Self

Each of us is more than just flesh and blood and bone. We are beings of pure light, held to this plane by the flesh and blood and bone vessel we experience this plane through. We are all something greater, something more. I will do my best to put into words that which cannot ever be truly described.

Imagine the night sky. It is full of stars, planets, comets, and other celestial bodies. All these that are seen are of one galaxy. The Galaxy stretches on hundreds light-years in all directions from where you are right now. However, our galaxy is not the only galaxy. It is one of an unknown, possibly infinite number of galaxies in a possibly-infinite universe. Each star is part of their system, and each system a part of their galaxy, and each galaxy a part of the universe.

Now, I am sure that has made you feel smaller than you can even fathom. Do not let it, because you must remember that everything that exists is made of energy, it is made of qi. You, me, the computer, the planet, the stars, the galaxies, and everything that is in the universe. It is all qi or emptiness. You are part of this energy, of this universal force. This energy has a higher state of consciousness, and each of its creations can access this higher consciousness, including the human race. All it takes is recognizing it is there. Your mind's focus determines your reality. If you believe in the higher self, you will have no problem finding it. If you are skeptical, it will be much harder...but that does not mean it is impossible.

We must first examine how we are linked to this higher self. Imagine now a big ball of string. This ball is infinitely bigger than anything you have ever seen. It is made up of an unknown numbers of strands, all forming into one big mass. Now, see the ends of each strand straying off and having a small bead tied on the end. That bead represents each of the things in creation. You are one of those beads, tied to the end of a strand of this massive ball of string. You are a part of it, and through it, you are a part of all other life. To know this is the first step to being able to live in the higher self.

The next step is to learn to look inwards for answers. This can be done through various ways. The most common ways are trancing or through meditation. Trancing is a little difficult to explain, so I will use the example of meditation. As you meditate, you quiet all your questions or concerns, your stresses, your worries. Clear them all. Then, actively distance yourself from all those things that make you who you are. Remove your ego, your emotions, your worries, your concerns, your personality, your entire uniqueness. You must return to the state at which you are in harmony with the higher self. When you are separate from who you were, you are nothing more than your inner self. Your inner self is the string, whereas all that you just stripped away was the bead, covering the end of the string. Your inner self is merely an extension of the higher self. To reach that level is to have the full understanding of the universal consciousness at your disposal.

That is not all there is to living in the higher self. We must do what we can, as humans, to stray from our human tendencies, and to stay as close to our inner self as we can, so that our outer self and inner self are not fighting with one another for control of the self, and you can be more readily open to the higher self.

Living in the higher self is living selflessly. It brings about a defined sense of purpose, and a greater understanding of people, things, and the workings of the universe. This takes many years to reach, but the path does not end there. As you reach the higher self, you must do all you can to honor the guidance of the higher self. Honor that which is all life and all things. Treat it with the utmost respect, not merely as some weird esoteric fluke. It is that which is above all.

The Way of the Sword

People take up the practice of the sword for a multitude of reasons. Some for exercise, others for the technical skills honed by its use: timing, distance, and courage to name but a few. There are others who take up the sword to learn about such an integral, intimate part of the Japanese way of living. Some undertake the training of the weapon as a form of advanced flowing meditation. While each of these aims are fully attainable, they are not the true Way of the Sword. Only in the pursuit of the four, and more still, can the true way be seen.

There are teachings of two different swords: the *satsujinken*, or the death-dealing sword; and the *katsujinken*, or the life-giving sword. This is not meant for one to feel as if they are two separate blades, made for different reasons; but rather the in and yo (yin and yang) of each blade. Both 'sides' of the sword are used to unmake evil. Also, just as the Chinese yin/yang diagram, each holds the seed of its compliment.

The *Satsujinken* is the blade of combat. It is the blade of the bujutsu. The death-dealing sword is the razor edge of tempered steel, working with lethal grace.

The *Katsujinken* is the blade of meditation. Is it the sword of budo. The life-giving sword is the back of the blade, kept at a mirror shine, and always looking back at its wielder.

However, these roles are not absolute. The sword of death is used to save, at least, your own life... if not countless others. The sword of life, also seemingly contrary to its nature, is use to destroy one's ego, killing your outer shell, and reveal your true nature and design. To follow the Way of the Sword is to know both the *satsujinken* and the *katsujinken* at once, each held in the balance of the katana, meshed endlessly into the other, as the folds of the *shinken*.

There is a common samurai concept: to live by the sword is to die by the sword. This sentiment has, to it, many layers. On the surface, this is a truthful statement as to the life of a career warrior. To live for battle is to die in battle. It is the nature of conflict that, given time, one will eventually fall in direct combat. As mentioned above, to live in the Way of the Sword is also to destroy the outer shell of the ego. To remove greed, desire, and other such worldly longings, all traits of the ego, does to 'kill' the person who longed for such things and pleasures. To truly live by the sword is also to do so for the rest of one's life. It is to allow the changes brought about through training, and to live by them for the total length of one's days. These are but a few layers.

《》《》《》《》《》

REVELATIONS

Such an ominous title, in this Judeo-Christian dominated worldview, but I have no other way to put it. One day, I was standing on my mom's back porch, talking to my by-then step-father about something callous my Dad had done. I cannot remember what it was, but I know it was immature for such a seasoned old guy. I had done my best to forgive him of the wrongs he had done to me. He had finally seen a doctor and was put on anti-depressants, which had made him a totally different person. I saw that all his anger and aggression towards me was meant for himself, but he did not have the tools to deal with it. He did what he knew how to do, lash out. I just happened to be the primary target at the time.

Anyway, I had told this trivial piece of stupid to my Mom, and astonished by the lack of logic found in the action, asked for the hundredth or so time, expecting the same answer as usual, "Is he really my father?". Of course, if the answer was "yes", then this would be kind of pointless to tell, wouldn't it? Obviously, the truth finally surfaced, and the answer was "no".

Have you ever been hit by a car, or taken a strong punch to the center of the chest? I've had both over the years. They stun you, a lot. Yeah, this stun was a great deal harder. Imagine a meteor landing on your soul. This wasn't just a blow delivered to the body. This was a sledgehammer taken to the crystalline form of my paradigm, my life. All the sudden, my brothers were only half-brothers, and folk I had grown up thinking of as family, weren't anymore. It explained why I looked nothing like Dad, everyone thought it was simply due to having a lower metabolism. My brothers, they look like him, the older more so than the younger. It also explained something I had read during my occult studies that had baffled my mind. The saying was that first-born children were treated better in most old civilizations was because they inherited the power of the family. This is also why younger siblings were led by the first born. It was a point of privilege in that they were the most gifted, from the occult point of view. It turns out, I am the first born of my true father, whom I will call Bob for the purposes of this text, and the only born of my parents together.

I found out I was the product of two affairs, Mom and Bob worked together, and both found an escape from their unhappy marriages in one another. This changed the equation totally. The one person whom I thought I could trust totally had spent my entire life hiding the truth. The dynamic between myself and my abuser made me question if he knew, or even suspected. Who was this man who was supposed to be my father? It turned out, I had two more half-siblings, another brother, and his older sister. I was invisible to their lives, Bob's secret which he could not verify, and had all but forgotten by the time I found him.

Learning about who Bob was beat me up more than learning he existed. Everything I had that made me special, that set me apart from my brothers, came from him. The bipolar disorder was a by-product of his diagnosed depression. My unrelenting ego, pride, and anger as well, in that his depression was sadistic, not masochistic. My intellect, also a trait of my true origins. My affinity to martial arts and energetics came from a man who spent several years of his life before my birth training in Hapkido, a Korean version of Japan's most famed internal combat art, Aikido. My love of philosophy and religious faith came from a man who lived by the Code of Christ. Firearms, sense of humor, receding hairline that I had shaved off a year prior, writing, musical talent... all of it came from *him*.

Indeed, you see a crisis of identity forming. I remember feeling joy at this new circumstance that I had begged for all my life. I remember feeling rage for how I was treated growing up. Mostly, I remember feeling lost. Everything I had built was built on a foundation of lies. The idea of a father had become a sour taste in my mouth, after all the betrayals I had suffered by those whom I placed in that role. I hated them, all of them, whether they knew or not. I remember Tank asked me what I would do if he did not want to get to know me, to acknowledge me. I remember the snarl, the disgust, as I said "If not, I've already had enough that have rejected me, fuck him. What's one more?"

My training had dissolved away when all my preconceptions of myself fell apart. All I had left was selfishness, hatred, and a lust to live a life that would *make* Bob reject me, a cruel intent to make him abandon me. Something in me wanted to show him how wrong I was, so

I could make it all his fault. I have never been the person I was since that moment. The idea lasted a great deal longer than I like to admit, but I am no longer trying to make him reject me.

Well, I met Bob for the first time three months after I found out about him, about myself. He was timid, nervous. I was angry, judgmental. It was not a good meeting. After our meal, I went outside and lit a cigarette. He made some comment about making me give up that bad habit. I remember the thought of *Who the hell does he think he is, telling me, a grown man, what I can and cannot do with my time, money, and health?* Yeah, I was losing everything. It was several months before I realized it, too. Downward spirals get faster the longer you are in one. My brothers found out, and I felt the change in them for a time, but it was brief and has gone. I grew a distrust for Mom, knowing that she had been keeping such great and terrible secrets from me for so long. I began to shut out my entire family, so I found a new one.

Well, founded it a better word, but co-founded is more truthful. Tank and I began our Clan, a social club of people who just didn't really fit. It was built off the motorcycle club paradigm, just without the vehicular requirements. We often say we are a group of misfits that fit together perfectly. I remember the fires I went through during the creation of our Clan, some of them social, some political, most of them personal. The formation of this Club brought an entire new point of separation from me and my relatives. Many did not understand its purpose, some were even antagonistic about it. These fires burned away my weaknesses, and the only time I felt happy was when I was with the Club, and often times, even that was only skin deep. In time, as the Club grew, I stopped seeing the members as friends, and rather as family. That is why I call them my Clan. We are brothers, not by blood, because you cannot choose your genetics. No, we are brothers in an entirely different fashion. They became my spiritual family, and I am insanely thankful for them. I do not know where I would be without them.

Through them, I saw that I would be accepted, no matter who or what I was. My relationship with Bob became sporadic at its best, and emotionally volatile more than once, but that did not matter to them. I was still me, and I had found who I was. I had become the future me I had seen all those years ago. I was still Jedi, am still Jedi, but I was no longer the drone. I had found my voice, on the Path, and in life. Life had become my Path, and my Clan is the reason for this unity.

After our first year as a formal Club, I realized I had dedicated myself to the foundation and expansion of this grouping, and it had succeeded. I began to see a spark in myself I had not for a long time. I looked back at my past, evident looking around my room at all the trinkets and treasures that had come to be mine as part of my growth. Wand, chalice, dagger, and stone sat on a shelf, above that a statue of Buddha and my lightsaber. My collection of swords sat on a shrine next to those shelves. My boxing bag still stood in my room, my gi hung with care in the closet. My martial arts books, and metaphysics books sat on the top two shelves of my bookcase, huddled over three shelves filled with my faith, and the fiction it had come to me in. My library of my version of Aesop's fables, each one telling me one more piece of the Path I have been on since I was twelve.

It was then that I asked myself, what is next on my Path of the Jedi? I had attained the level of Master in the philosophy of the Path. I had attained a level of mastery in the combative aspect of the Arts. I had also already earned a Doctorate in Metaphysics. I was Ordained, with a Doctorate in Divinity. None of this was free sign-up-and-done stuff, either. These took work. Now, I know there is no such thing as total mastery, but I knew the Path wasn't just practice and perfection. I knew in my bones it was far from over. I searched esoteric texts to see if their upper echelons would give me any clues. They didn't, big surprise. Not sure what else to do, I began a nightly vigil of charging a bottle of water with the energy I had felt during each of my revelations on the Path thus far. The wonder and awe, the humility, the passion, the fever of learning how to understand. I asked the Force every night, for months, to reveal to me the next step.

Finally, it did. The vigil idea was a step handed to me by the Force. This is what I do now. I live within the Five Pillars. They are what hold the Path together, even when those on it dwindle to nothing, or degrade to petty children. I found the Thirty-three Stones of the Way. Stones as in stepping stones. One of them, I finish now, with this last bit. I am telling my tale.

The 5 Pillars of the Jedi Way
Honor
Patience
Humility
Faith
Justice

The 5 Failures along the Jedi Way
Greed
Haste
Arrogance
Doubt
Malice

The 5 Steps to Jedi Wisdom
Focus
Introspection
Rectitude
Bravery
Meditation

The 33 Stones of the Jedi Way

These steps along the Path were revealed to me by the Force. Steps 1–13 are required to happen either in the order listed, or close to it. Step 14–31 are labeled oddly, in that they can start at any point after Step 1. They are separate in that they have no set order of which they build upon one another. The only point is that all of the first 31 must take place before Step 32 can take proper hold, which has to happen before Step 33, which is why the last two are also numbered.

I will present them in an outline, then do my best to describe these steps as the Force has given them to me. I may not fully understand them yet, so do with them what you see fit.

1. "I am the Force."
2. Unhooking the Ego
3. There is no Dark "Side"
4. The Force Triquetra
5. Meditation as a Way of Life
6. Physical Discipline
7. Expand the Mind
8. Trial by Fire
9. Connection to All
10. Inner Alchemy
11. Breaking through the Veil
12. Resonance
13. "I am the Keep."

14–31, no set order

-Point of View
-Cruelty as Kindness
-Eyes of the Force
-Hearing the Whispers
-Opening the Inner Eye
-Disconnect
-To Move Beyond
-Return to the Root
-Tell your Tale
-Guide, not Guru
-Spirit in the Force
-Forge your Sword
-The Whet Stone
-Becoming the Emotions
-Finding the Key
-Walking Between Worlds
-Compassionate World
-Seeing the Forest beyond the Trees

32. Crystallize
33. Avatar

The 33 Stones are not to be viewed solely as stepping stones, where you use its sturdy surface to guide you beyond it, and you are done. They are also to be seen as the stones of a crystal healer, each kept safe close to the body of the Path Walker. Each step we take must become part of us forever, or we cannot move forward.

----

1. "I am the Force."

This point is the start of the Path. This is when one understands that they are built of the Force, their minds are an extension of the Force, and that their entire existence, from their physical shell to their lifetime of experiences, are all of the Force. It is as if we exist in a dream of the Force, created totally by it, in every detail.

When one realizes this, they can find peace in knowing that not just all of their life, but all of every life, is the Force. There can be nothing outside of the Force.

2. Unhooking the Ego

Much of human suffering is caused by the ego. It is the barrier between a person, and the purity of the Force. With the ego constantly screaming its hot, its cold, I'm hungry, I'm tired, its too loud, etc. at us, we can calm the mind and feel the flow of the Force. For the ego, the Force is not for us. It is what separates us from our spiritual heritage. The ego thinks we must worship the Force, in whatever facet it sees by whatever name that facet is known. If we do not worship, we are not worthy of even a whisper of the Force, and this keeps us disconnected.

Unhooking the ego begins when we learn to think with the pure mind, not concerned with the trivial nature of material life. We cannot banish the ego, or we lose all sense of self, thus losing the purpose of the experience of life. It is at this point that we can evaluate what type of person our ego is. The Jedi Code is an amazing tool to help to quiet the ego, remove its hooks from your mind, and allow you to begin to see beyond yourself.

3. There is no Dark "Side"

The Force is. Period. Always has been, always will be. It will not change simply because someone attempts to make it do so. The Force does not have a dark side of its own. The darkness that possesses the Force in some is their own darkness. We exist in and of the Force, but the Darkness is Malice, a side-effect of the ego driven separate-existance point of view. Is there evil? Yes. Does evil exist within the Force? Yes, but only in that those who do evil are just as much of the Force as those who do good.

4. The Force Triquetra

This refers to the triple state of the human experience of all things. We live in three dimensions, and out existence has three dimensions as well. We have the body, the mind, and the spirit. The Force relates to us within our three-phase view of reality. It speaks to each part of us. Realize that these are not separate energies, simply separate parts of the same energy. They are simply three facets of a much, much larger stone.

The Living Force is the energy that makes up all living things. It is the energy of matter, the bioelectricity that makes your nerves and brain work, that allow you to read this, now. The Living is the most prominent energy felt, being that all things share a part of its vibration. All things hold a memory, and at leave a minor spark of life. Even a stone has some life to it. It is a part of the Living World, and a part of the Force. This is the Body.

The Guiding Force is the energy that makes up thought, more specifically intuition. This is the first vibration to be felt by people, even if they hold no concept of the Force, in part or as much of the whole as we can experience. It comes when least expected, and it gives insight into the celestial memory of all things, a phenomenon known as the Akashic Records. This the Mind.

The Uniting Force, also called the Unifying Force, is that of our highest spiritual vibration on this plane. It is was shows each of us that we are bigger than we seem, that we are all connected. This is the Spirit.

The Triquetra has become a symbol of Catholicism to describe the Holy Trinity: the father (the mind), the son (the body), and the Holy Ghost (the spirit). This symbol is a blueprint to our existence in the Force. Those who view the facet of the Force known as the Judeo-Christian religions see that each person was made in the image of their creator. That image, the Triquetra, is the blueprint for spiritual life. When the three parts act separately, there is no balance. When brought together, they time in an endless knot to show the unity of all.

5. Meditation as a Way of Life

Meditation comes in countless forms, with varied intention between one technique to the next. They all hold one thing in common, stopping the chatter of the ego, clearing the pure mind of mindless dribble and complaints. Meditation is what allows us to truly think, and feel, and sense the Force. We become more able to feel the lack of balance in our bodies. We can feel a weakness of muscle, or a discomfort in the digestive track. We can release tension of the body, and help to correct the flow of the Living energy within ourselves to find true balance.

6. Physical Discipline

We must not only understand our physical shell, but care for it as well. We are able to prolong and improve our lives. This is done by taking a physical discipline. Many within the Jedi will think this means a martial art. For my path, and many others like me, it does. The martial arts are by far my personal recommendation, but they are not the only way. Some may just take up a diet, others an exercise routine. It could simply be stretching. Running, yoga, tae bo, boxing, competitive jump-roping, pilates, spinning. Whatever. Some way to improve the body and fight the ego's desire to quit, that is what this is about.

7. Expand the Mind

The human mind is a wondrous thing, capable of dreaming infinitely complex things. Inventing new ways to help the world, or way to destroy it. It all comes from knowledge, as the Code says. When we take in new knowledge, we combine it with what we already know, intellectually and intuitively. This helps us to get a larger grasp of the world around us. The more you learn intellectually, the more intuitive connections you will build from one point to the other, even if they have nothing in common. This is the macrocosm or existence seen in the microcosm of your life.

8. Trial by Fire

This is not something you have to actively search out, it will find you. It may be a physical altercation, it may be a shaking of your faith, it may be some perception-shattering revelation. It has to happen, there is no way around it. If we do not have ourselves tested, we will never know our strengths or weaknesses. This test, once done one, can reappear infinitely between now and the final Stone on the Path. It is not enough to pass the first test, but to welcome the trials you will receive for the rest of your days.

9. Connection to All

This comes from the solidifying of the united aspect of all life. You will begin to realize your true level of intuitive knowledge as it is fed to you from the Force.

10. Inner Alchemy

This is an expansion of the physical discipline. We all get better at what we focus on, but that is not the point of this. We must take ourselves apart, and rebuild ourselves, time and again, to purify ourselves. "Solve et Coagula", the dissolve and coagulate, to take apart and bind together. Inner Alchemy is done to remove imperfections in our bodies, our minds, our spirits. It is a form of introspective purification, and vitally needed.

11. Breaking through the Veil

This step is to learn that there is more life, more sentience, in the Force than what we experience in our daily lives. Call them what you will, angels, demons, fae, dragons, spirit guides, ghosts, totems, gremlins, or whatever. They are on this plane, just beyond our own vibrations, and they interact with us, called to us by our use of the Force. They may even cause problems, if you ignore some of the more mischievous ones. We have to learn to experience them on their levels, and thus we must raise our own energetic vibration enough to see beyond the cloak of darkness that stops us from seeing further.

12. Resonance

The Resonance is a point where we find the ability to bring our vibrations in tune with our surroundings at all times. Often time, those who walk the Path do not allow their energy to change from one place to the next, and thus some places give us headaches, while others bring us elation. It is not a stain on the area, but the difference of vibration acting upon our own energies.

13. "I am the Keep."

This tenets expands on the first step of "I am the Force". It is reached when you learn to armor yourself with the Force. It is the sustaining energy found in lengthy fasting, or the energy warriors project that give them the aura of invincibility. The faith and understanding of the Force is steeped high into the walker of the Path, and they are all the more able Jedi for it. Intuition becomes as natural as logic, and it becomes hard to learn the difference. It is the calm power exuded from a monk of a meditative path. It is the key to the last line of the Jedi Code, proclaiming that there is no death. This ties greatly into the samurai ideal of living as if already dead. It gives disregard to injury, as all that can be destroyed in the body, not the spirit. The Force protects the Inner Self from ever dying.

14-31, no set order
-Point of View

This stone is about learning to see with our hearts, and view every side of a problem, often understanding the persons involved far better than we should. It also teaches us to see our own faults and imperfections by viewing ourselves outside of our own head. We learn to understand ourselves, and by knowing our reasons for doing things, we learn why others do what they do.

-Cruelty as Kindness

Perhaps seen as a negative ideal, this Step is very needed. Compassion and service are the call of a Jedi in their daily life. However, this teaches us that at times, the most helpful thing we can do is nothing at all. Aiding those who can not manage for themselves is our charter, not aiding those who do not wish the sizzle of their own complacence. When one has the strength to act, and we help them instead, we do them a disservice by allowing them to maintain the mask of weakness.

–Eyes of the Force
This speaks of seeing into the past, the present, and the flow of time of possible futures. This helps us to see any past lives some part of our souls were found in. It helps us to see the past events surrounding a person, place, or even an item. It helps us to see into the depths of a situation as it is happening, and see the currents of time. It helps us to break through the certainty of now, and swim in the currents of what can be. We often will see what is most likely to happen, unless we are looking for some specific occurrence. Our ego will make us see what we want to find, and it is hard to tell what we see of our desire or of higher revelation.

–Hearing the Whispers
This speaks of a great many skills the Jedi can begin to develop very early. It is not empathy, for that is just interpreting emotional energy of another person. This can be hearing the thoughts of someone else, or a calling from the Force itself. It is the voice of the Force, made into words by the nature of our pure mind.

–Opening the Inner Eye
The inner Eye is a tool that can make a Jedi far more intuitive than either of the two above Stones. This refers to the moments of enlightened understanding, flashes of what is know as *satori* to the Japanese. When you have a moment of the Inner Eye

opening, you feel your endless connection, feeling your infinitely huge spirit and your microscopic physical shell at the same time.

-Disconnect
To disconnect is to take inventory in who you have become. You step back from all of it for a time, the Path, the Force, the Jedi, the development of the spirit. You shed your higher connection, and take a hard look at your person.

-To Move Beyond
To Move Beyond is an extension of Breaking through the Veil. It is not enough that a Jedi know the base energetic arts taught on the Path. We must all take into consideration abilities we do not readily teach. Reiki, spellwork, shamanism, crystal healing, the various forms of divination, the list is nearly endless. We move beyond just the Jedi ideal to better understand the Force, how it reacts to various methods, and how it has been seen by the peoples of the world for as much as we have record.

-Return to the Root
This step usually happens after the step listed previous, but not necessarily. Once we have an enhanced grasp of how the Force works, we throw it all out, returning to the Roots of our development, the Jedi Way. During the process, you may realize you hang on to some of the techniques of other sects, such as using crystals or a staff. That is fine, as the Path is rigid, but the Way unique.

-Tell your Tale
To gain a better understanding of yourself, and your path, it is good to periodically tell your personal tale. You don't have to show it to anyone, so be as harsh as you need to be. Tell your

history as you remember it, because if you do not remember it, it did not make a lasting impact on your development.

–Guide, not Guru
Part of the development of a Jedi is to pass on your knowledge and experience. Each person has their own unique story to tell, and their own unique lessons to teach. The trick is, more often than not, when we first start teaching, we forget that we learned from other people. Knowing how our own experiences have helped to mold us, and the bone-deep knowing that your Path fits you, we begin to discount the teachings of our fellow generation of Jedi. We begin to act as if we are the supreme right answer, and we don't do it on purpose. To have someone look up to you for your understanding, the ego begins to make us feel like we are the supreme conduit of the Force, when our experience is just one of infinite facets.

–Spirit in the Force
This is the point where we connect to the Force so much that we feel its glow in our spirit. We stop simply trusting the Force, and begin to live in the flow of the Force. It is hard to put into exact words, but once this step is attained, it is very simply recognized.

–Forge your Sword
This step has a thousand meaning, but the largest of them is to find the weapon that fits you best and make it your own. For some, this may be an actual sword, whereas for others it may mean to carve a staff, or to sharpen the mind. If your means of defense is through brute strength and combat skill, it can mean to forge your body into a living weapon. Mostly, for me, it refers to my empty-handed combative skills.

-The Whet Stone

This may seem like an extension of the step listed above, and while it is closely related, they are different. The purpose of this step is to ready your spirit for the rigors of acting in defense. Whatever your weapon, the Whet Stone hones that weapon into a shape and edge you are not only able to use, but prepared to use as well.

-Becoming the Emotions

This point refers to the act of release the subjugation of the emotions. This is a dangerous step, if one has not properly learned to unhook the ego, or control their reactions. As such, this step, if taken deliberately, should be done later in one's training. If it happens of circumstance, then handle it as best you can. Allow yourself to feel all of your emotions as they emanate into the Force around you. Bring to mind points of joy, moments of maddening rage, supreme ecstasy, bleeding sorrow, and true peace. The process of feeling the total strength of the emotions is that, through the training along the path, we each change, and our emotions change with us. Emotions are bitten down on in early training to help us keep our center, so that we may learn the strength of the Force, and allow the teachings of un-attachment, different from detachment, to bring us the strength to handle our most chaotic aspects.

-Finding the Key

This refers to finding the path that bridges intellect and intuition. It is as if one has unlocked a door they did not know could ever be opened. Thinking will get faster, and you will know things you never knew you had learned. It is called by many finding the Akashic Records. It is a level beyond Expand the Mind, where the mind is now as big as it will ever get. Meditation will be second-nature to you, and you will begin to see the infinite existence, rather than a mere concept of it.

–Walking Between Worlds

This Stone refers not to just breaking the veil, and being able to interact beyond this world, but existing as one's self in both at once, straddling the metaphorical line between the two. Communicating as readily with earthly beings as with otherworldly being, so as to use the insight given by the pair.

–Compassionate World

The meaning behind this Stone revolves around the Law of Sympathetic Return, a Hermetic Law. It does not mean the world is always going to be compassionate to you, your woes, or your desires. It means, what you strive for, the Force gives you. The key word is strive. Not plan, want, or dream for. Wants are driven by the ego. Plans are just an idea. Dreams are wasted without action. You get what you need, and what you work for. Hope is an illusion to comfort the ego, telling it "it could happen". The Force, and by extension, the world we all live in, gives you a paycheck. You get what you earn, and you earn what you get.

–Seeing the Forest beyond the Trees

This is a very important revelation, which is why I decided to list it last among the un-numbered. Some will get this very early, more will not. I was one that it took far too long with. The training of a Jedi takes on three major parts: the philosophical branch, the Path; the physical/metaphysical branch, the Arts: and the religio-spiritual branch, the Way. Together, when fused into one cohesive unit, truly forming the Way by making the Arts and the Path spiritual in nature, we start to truly become Jedi. It is only though this that we can achieve greater than what we are.

32. Crystallize

This step seems kind of redundant, but it is a very needed thing. It is at this point that we review our lives, and our training, to see that we have made every step thus far in the Path. Yes, the inventory is a very major part, and we must be truthful in this self-evaluation. The True Mind will know if each stone has been taken, and collected. The ego will tell you right away that they have, so if you do not question that, go back to Unhooking the Ego. Meditate on what you have learned. If you have trouble, return to Meditation as a Way of Life. This evaluation can show you your flaws, your holes, and your frayed edges. As the Oracle of Delphi said, Know Thyself. Be true to yourself, or you only harm yourself.

33. Avatar

This is a point reached when all the previous steps have been taken, and collected. It is through a great deal of self-sacrifice and self-evaluation, and almost masochistic levels of Inner Alchemy, to make yourself the epitome of the Jedi you are meant to be, the Jedi Avatar.

The Path of Knowledge

Shu: Copy
Ha: Learn
Ri: Transcend

Shu-ha-ri is the way of All.

We copy our teachers, in mannerisms, technique, and behavior. This is Shu, the first stage of learning.

We copy until the trait is imprinted upon us, making it part of who we are. This is Ha, the second stage of learning.

We learn of ourselves until we break the mold of our teachers, no longer letting their trait imprint upon us, but allowing ourselves to imprint upon the trait. This is Ri, the transcendence.

Shu-ha-ri is done infinitely, time and again, until we leave this world. Shu is the Student, Ha is the Adept, Ri is the Master. Shuhari is the Avatar.

The Avatar is the most refined crystalline form of the Way. The Avatar is found in and beyond the Shu-ha-ri, in the Path of the Inner Alchemist. "Solve et Coagula", to dissolve and coagulate: to break down and refine only to rebuild in the more crystalline form, further purified until the resonance is found. This is found by taking the revelations of the Ri stage, and forgetting it for a time, so that you become your own teacher, and treat it as the Shu, for futher refinement and revelation.

As this process of personal re-education moves ever forward, the Master becomes more than a master of the self, but a Master of the Way, an Avatar, a purified example of what it means to walk the Path, train in the Arts, and live in the Way. The example is found in that the Avatar is ever-growing, always in a state of personal refinement through the principles of internal alchemy, Solve et Coagula.

In time, it is said the Avatar becomes not just an example of the Way, but becomes the Way itself. Then, they have reached the pinnacle if development, the apex of the Path. They become the Ascended, no longer just an Avatar of the Way, but an Avatar of the Force itself. No longer are they troubled by the draw of the Inner Darkness, for they have divorced themselves from Malice, the key to the dark. No longer do they push against their own nature, for their nature has formed into the truth of the Way.

《》《》《》《》《》

FAR FROM OVER

My tale ends here, now. That is because I am here, now.
By the time you read this, there might be still more to write,
but that will have to wait for another day.

Allow me to finish this with my thanks. I want to thank
everyone that has ever taught me anything, whether
mentioned here or not. If you are reading this, likely you
helped me to learn and develop. Next, I want to express
my hope. If you do not know me beyond these pages, I
hope you found in my tale whatever brought you to it. I do
not write this to convert anyone to the Jedi Path. That is
not our Way.

Finally, I would like to challenge every Jedi to do as I have
done. Perhaps not bound, page by page, but follow the
Stones, and tell your tale. You will be amazed at how
much you have changed.

I do what I do, and have done what I have done, because
it was and is the Will of the Force. I am, as all Jedi are at
there core, a Servant of the Force.

May the Force keep you safe for your journey.

Printed in Great Britain
by Amazon

40071686R00139